PUB WALKS

IN

Lincolnshire

Other areas covered in the Pub Walks series include:

Bedfordshire
Berkshire
Birmingham & Coventry
Bristol and Bath
Buckinghamshire
Cambridgeshire
Cheshire
The Chilterns
The Cotswolds
South Cumbria
Dartmoor & South Devon
Derbyshire
Essex
West Essex
Exmoor & North Devon
Gloucestershire
Herefordshire
Hertfordshire
The Isle of Wight
Lancashire
Leicestershire and Rutland

Middlesex & West London
Midshires Way
Norfolk
Northamptonshire
Nottinghamshire
Oxfordshire
Shropshire
Staffordshire
Suffolk
Surrey
The Surrey Hills
The Thames Valley
North Wales
South Wales
Warwickshire
Wiltshire
Worcestershire
East Yorkshire
North Yorkshire
South Yorkshire
West Yorkshire

*A complete catalogue is available from the publisher at
3 Catherine Road, Newbury, Berkshire.*

PUB WALKS
IN
Lincolnshire

THIRTY CIRCULAR WALKS
AROUND LINCOLNSHIRE INNS

Brett Collier

COUNTRYSIDE BOOKS
NEWBURY, BERKSHIRE

First Published 1994
Reprinted 1995

Revised and updated 1998

© Brett Collier 1994

COUNTRYSIDE BOOKS
3 Catherine Road
Newbury, Berkshire

ISBN 1 85306 300 2

Designed by Mon Mohan
Cover illustration by Colin Doggett
Photographs and maps by the author

Produced through MRM Associates Ltd., Reading
Typeset by Paragon Typesetters, Queensferry, Clwyd
Printed and bound in England by Woolnough Bookbinders,
Wellingborough

Contents

Introduction   10

Walk 1   Greatford: The Hare and Hounds (2¼ or 4½ miles)   12

      2   Deeping St James: The Waterton Arms (2½ miles)   16

      3   Castle Bytham: The Castle Inn (2¼ miles)   20

      4   Dyke: The Wishing Well (3 miles)   24

      5   Pinchbeck: The Ship (4 miles)   27

      6   Gedney Drove End: The Rising Sun (3¼ miles)   31

      7   Harlaxton: The Gregory Arms (2 or 3¼ miles)   34

      8   Old Somerby: The Fox and Hounds (2¼ miles)   38

      9   Newton: The Red Lion (4½ miles)   41

     10   Aswarby: The Tally Ho Inn (4½ miles)   45

     11   Anton's Gowt: The Oak Tree (¾ or 3 miles)   49

     12   Coleby: The Bell Inn (2½ miles)   52

     13   Tattersall Thorpe: The Blue Bell (1¾ miles)   56

     14   Southrey: The Riverside Inn (3¼ miles)   60

     15   Dunholme: The Four Seasons (1½ or 3½ miles)   64

     16   Minting: The Sebastopol Inn (1½ miles)   68

     17   Belchford: The Blue Bell (4½ miles)   72

     18   South Thoresby: The Vine Inn (2 or 3½ miles)   76

19	Tealby: The King's Head (3½ miles)	80
20	Donington on Bain: The Black Horse (1¼, 2¼ or 3½ miles)	84
21	Louth: The Wheatsheaf (3 miles)	88
22	Little Cawthorpe: The Royal Oak (1½ miles)	92
23	Theddlethorpe All Saints: The King's Head (3¾ miles)	96
24	Saltfleet: The New Inn (2¾ miles)	100
25	Susworth: The Jenny Wren (4½ miles)	104
26	Nettleton: The Salutation Inn (4 miles)	108
27	Barnoldby le Bec: The Ship Inn (4 miles)	112
28	Burton upon Stather: The Sheffield Arms (3 miles)	116
29	Barrow Haven: The Haven Inn (2 miles)	120
30	East Halton: The Black Bull (4¼ miles)	124

Publisher's Note

We hope that you obtain considerable enjoyment from this book; great care has been taken in its preparation. However, changes of landlord and actual closures are sadly not uncommon. Likewise, although at the time of publication all routes followed public rights of way or well-established permitted paths, diversion orders can be made and permissions withdrawn.

We cannot accept responsibility for any inaccuracies, but we are anxious that all details covering both pubs and walks are kept up to date, and would therefore welcome information from readers which would be relevant to future editions.

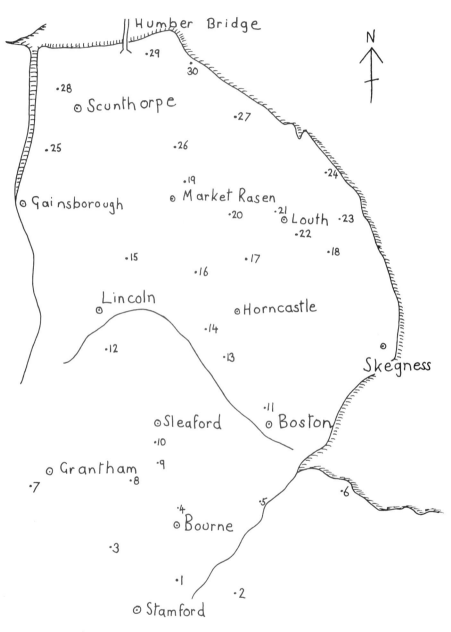

Area map showing locations of the walks.

Introduction

The book covers the sparsely populated 'old Lincolnshire', from the Humber to the Wash. The pace of life can be slow here and there are miles and miles of empty field paths waiting to be explored, with lots of space under wide horizons, be it farmland, heathland, wold, fen or salt marsh. Lincolnshire is supposed not to have any scenery at all and has been said to be dull, flat and uninteresting. However, you will find for yourself that the very size of the county means that there is a range of scenery and geographical features difficult to match elsewhere in lowland Britain.

There are also inns and pubs to be discovered in villages with incredible names such as Anton's Gowt, Barnoldby le Bec, Burton upon Stather, Gedney Drove End and many more. During your walks and explorations you will find that the Romans were here, followed by the Vikings and each of them left their mark upon roads, dykes, villages and towns. In the Second World War Lincolnshire became 'Bomber County' and even today OS maps show the outline of many a wartime airfield and there is still plenty of evidence on the ground of the influence of the RAF upon the county. The effect of the Beeching destruction of rural railway routes may also be seen only too clearly in the sketch maps of some of the walks.

As a result of the relaxation of licensing laws, pubs no longer keep traditional opening hours and therefore I have indicated for each pub its normal pattern of opening, although some may keep different times for summer and winter. Meals are usually available from 12 noon until 2 pm, with 7 pm until 10 pm for evening meals, but some pubs have one day a week off when no meals are served. Many pubs now offer a 'traditional Sunday lunch' as a set meal on that day and may be unable to cope with bar snacks at the same time. It is wise to book meals in advance, certainly on Sundays and, in some cases, at any time over a weekend. The telephone number for each pub is given.

Most landlords have readily agreed that customers may leave their cars in the pub car park while they are doing the walk but it is only polite to warn the publican concerned that you are doing so. A strange car left in an empty car park outside normal opening hours could easily be treated with suspicion. A note left at the pub indicating your intention of returning to partake of their hospitality will certainly help to establish a good relationship. Further, as you are likely to be away some time, it is only courteous not to park immediately outside the main entrance.

The sketch maps, while perfectly adequate for each walk, cannot give you a full picture of the surrounding countryside and an OS map of the area will greatly add to your enjoyment and understanding of the countryside.

Changing out of walking boots, especially if they are muddy, is appreciated, for many country pubs are carpeted throughout nowadays. Dogs are sometimes permitted indoors but the majority of publicans are bound by hygiene regulations, which state that animals should not be present when food is being served.

The aim of the book is for you to enjoy Lincolnshire. In conclusion, I hope that it will bring you hours of good walking, for not only do the many miles of walks open up little-frequented countryside, but they also introduce you to the high quality of food and drink that is offered in these 30 inns.

Brett Collier

① Greatford
The Hare and Hounds

The low-beamed-ceiling building of the Hare and Hounds dates back to the 1740s, although it has been added to and developed many times since. The lounge has a stone-built fireplace with a huge barrel-shaped front and the walls are lined with a number of attractive oil and water-colour paintings, offered for sale by a local artist.

This pub aims to provide a warm, friendly atmosphere for the local community and visitors alike. It succeeds very well. Good, mostly home-cooked meals are available each day of the week, with dishes such as steak and ale pie and chilli con carne amongst some of the abiding favourites. In the evenings, meals are served in the dining room and main courses on the menu may include gammon steaks, and a selection of fish dishes including salmon, scampi and plaice. Local game is a speciality. The sweets range from spotted dick with custard, sponge pudding, cheesecake, and the ever popular Black Forest Gateau. meals are served seven days a week, lunchtimes and evenings. Well-kept beers on handpump include Wells Eagle, Wells Bombardier, Adnams Broadside, Morland Old Speckled Hen and Young's Winter Warmer. Ciders are Scrumpy Jack and Strongbow. Murphy's Stout and Red Stripe lager are also served. The dining-room is a no-smoking area and there are a number of picnic tables around the garden at the rear of the pub, with plenty of space for children to play.

The pub is open on Monday to Friday from 12 noon to 3 pm and from 5.30 pm to 11 pm, and on Saturday from 12 noon to 3 pm and 6 pm to 11 pm. Sunday 12 noon to 3 pm and 6 pm to 10.30 pm.

Telephone: 01778 560332.

How to get there: From the A6121 near Carlby turn eastwards to Greatford, which is 5 miles from both Stamford and Bourne, or from the A15 Market Deeping to Bourne road turn westwards across King Street (the Roman road) either at Baston or Langtoft.

Parking: A large car park is available at the pub but it would be courteous to tell the landlord if you are leaving you car while you walk. Limited roadside parking may be found in the village itself.

Length of the walk: 2¼ miles or 4½ miles. Map: OS Landranger sheet 130 Grantham and surrounding area (inn GR 086118).

Greatford, once famous for its watercress beds, is one of the most beautiful of South Kesteven's stone-built villages, with its attractive houses, unusual stone ornaments, splendid Elizabethan manor house, lovely church and small river. Kesteven existed long before the Domesday Book as a division of the shire when the kings of Wessex won back the Danelaw. The heathland region lying to the north of Stamford reaching up to Lincoln was heavily wooded and the term Kesteven includes an old British word for wood or forest. This delightful walk takes you through the village, across the Shillingthorpe Estate and alongside the infant West Glen river.

The Walk

Turn left out of the pub car park for a few yards only and then turn right across the bridge along the track leading to the church, with the attractive gardens and buildings of Greatford Hall on the left. After looking at the interesting church memorials and some of the inscriptions on the gravestones, go through the graveyard to the narrow path leading down to the West Glen river and on to the lane. Turn right at the lane, over the bridge, and continue to the junction with Main Street and the old school building on the left.

Cross Main Street to follow the signposted concrete footpath and, by another signpost, cross the rough paddock to a stile and waymark and go on to the bridge over a very wide drain. Cross the track leading

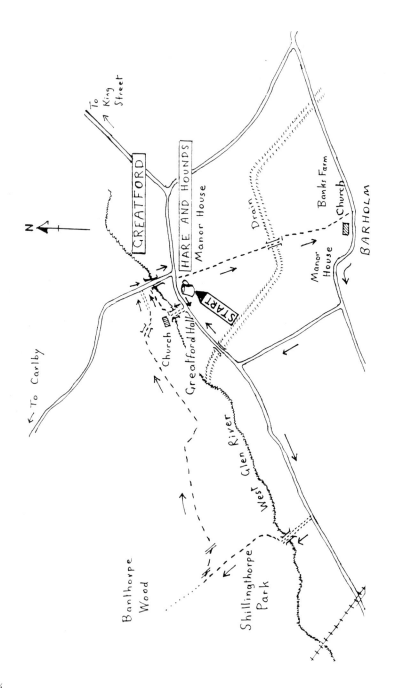

14

to Manor Farm buildings over on your right and continue forward towards Barholm church, with the hedge on your immediate left. Climb the slate stile, with the churchyard on your right, to turn right up the lane and follow the bends round, with Manor Farm on your right. Turn to the right along the quiet lane and continue for 700 yards to the T-junction into Greatford village, with traces of ridge and furrow ploughing on your right. Note the unusual 'The Steading' sign at the edge of the garden on your left.

For the longer walk: Turn left instead of right at the T-junction and continue for 1,000 yards. At the entrance to Shillingthorpe Park Estate, turn right up the drive on the signposted path with a stile at the side of the gate. Cross the bridge over the infant river and, 400 yards beyond the bridge, climb the first stile on your right to cross the small paddock to another stile in the right-hand corner. Cross the next field, just to the left of the three old trees, to an earth bridge over the dyke and a waymark.

Walk diagonally right to the field corner, with the small pond on your immediate right. Turn right for a few yards into the wood and proceed along a clear path with a stream over on the right. Cross the footbridge and bear right on the diverted, signposted path at the bottom of a garden. Turn left at the entry lane into Greatford Gardens development with the Greatford Estate boundary on your right. Upon reaching the road turn right into the village to follow your original route into Main Street and back to the car park.

Other places of interest: The Steam Brewery Museum at Stamford. Open from 10 am to 4 pm during the summer months. Telephone: 01780 52186.

2 Deeping St James
The Waterton Arms

This attractive pub, named after a local family, was built in 1600 with stone additions around 1800. There is an L-shaped bar with low beams, plain scrubbed tables, tile and flagged floors, a restaurant area, a public bar and a games room that is all sparklingly clean and neat. It has a marvellous atmosphere simply because it is so unspoilt.

This freehouse serves an incredible range of good, handpumped beer, including guest beers that change regularly. You could find Webster's Yorkshire Bitter, Fuller's Hock, Ruddles County and Best Bitter, Foster's Draught, John Smith's Bitter, Bass on draught, Craftsman Traditional Premium ale, Draught Guinness, Dry Blackthorn cider and Carlsberg lager. Bin ends are also on sale. There isn't a printed menu, for the choice of meals changes frequently. Large blackboards clearly indicate a wide range of foods, sufficient for all tastes, such as seafood pancakes, garlic mushrooms with cream or topped with Stilton, prawns harlequin, kidneys in mustard and cream with garlic bread, and gammon steaks with orange and Grand Marnier sauce. Vegetarian meals include cannelloni with ricotta and spinach. Fish dishes, such as king prawns in garlic or salmon en croûte, are also available. Children's meals are offered and the 'Lunchtime Extras' include omelettes, salads, jacket wedges and Barry's Bit on the Side. Children are welcome and there is a garden with a play area for them. There is also a patio with picnic tables but, as a policy, no segregated family room. Well-behaved dogs are permitted.

The pub is open on Monday to Friday from 11 am to 3 pm and 7 pm to 10 pm, and on Sunday from 12 noon to 2.30 pm and 7 pm to 10 pm. Saturday opening hours are 'all day', from 11 am to 11 pm. Meals are served at lunchtime and in the evenings throughout the week.

Telephone: 01778 342219.

How to get there: Deeping St James lies between Spalding and Stamford. Turn off the A16 (T) ½ mile east of Market Deeping and follow the secondary road (B1166) into the village.

Parking: There is ample parking at the side of the pub, with an overflow car park adjacent.

Length of the walk: 2½ miles. Map: OS Landranger sheet 142 Peterborough (inn GR 153094).

A surprisingly varied walk full of interest and ideal for anyone who is at all interested in rivers, water birds or churches. It is an easy stroll alongside the river Welland with the unusual, quiet Back Lane and a marvellous 850 year old priory church that is normally open.

The Walk

From the pub car park follow the small path through the children's play area, keeping the boundary hedge on your left. Go through the gate and turn left along the track. Upon reaching the road (Hereward Way), cross over and then turn right towards Bell Bridge. Continue straight forward past the bridge until you reach the Crown and Anchor pub and then cross the river Welland by the quaint, narrow bridge on High Lock. Turn left along the attractive embankment lane, with the river now on your left. Cross the road by the side of Bell Bridge (1651) to continue along the river side. At the road junction bear left for a few yards and at the bend in the road turn left on to a signposted path with a stile. The church dominates much of the walk and its size reflects its origins as a church connected to a monastic foundation. In this flat area it is said that it can be seen from 10 miles away.

Continue along this attractive path, following the bends in the river for almost a mile until you reach the Low Locks and a weir. Cross the river here and walk on to Eastgate. Go straight across the road and

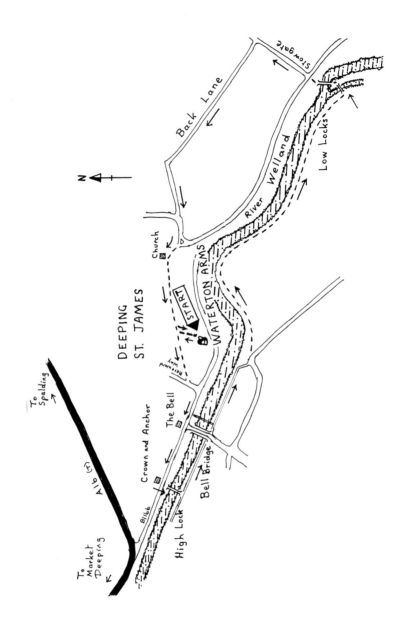

DEEPING ST. JAMES

N

To Spalding

A16 (T)

To Market Deeping

B1166

Crown and Anchor

The Bell

Bell Bridge

High Lock

Hereward Way

START

WATERTON ARMS

Church

Back Lane

River Welland

Low Locks

Stowgate

18

walk up Stowgate for about 200 yards. Turn left along Back Lane, with its intriguing narrow strips of gardens, and round the left-hand bend in the road towards the church. At the churchyard gate walk straight forward, leaving the village green triangle on your left and then turn right into the churchyard.

At the entrance to the church, walk straight forward, with the hall wall on your immediate left and the enormous cemetery on your right. At the path junction continue straight forward along the same track until you reach the path on your left leading back into the pub car park.

Castle Bytham
The Castle Inn

Today there are still two pubs in the village, but in former times there were seven and at least one of them may be seen during the walk. The Castle Inn is several hundred years old and it is reputed to possess a sealed passage leading to the mound where the castle motte and bailey formerly stood. Since 1973 the village has been a conservation area and many of the older houses are built of warm, grey local stone which was probably recycled after the destruction of the castle during the Wars of the Roses.

This fascinating inn is a freehouse, offering well-kept, handpumped Youngers Scotch Bitter, Mild and IPA, Theakston Best Bitter and Old Peculier, plus Murphy's Irish Stout, Gillespie's Malt Stout, McEwan and Beck's lagers and Scrumpy Jack cider. An excellent selection of home-cooked food is served every lunchtime and evening throughout the week in the open-plan, stone-built lounge bar, which has interesting inglenooks and, in season, a welcoming open fire. There is a blackboard menu, for dishes are constantly changing. In addition, there is a popular extensive à la carte menu available in the intimate restaurant every evening and at Sunday lunchtimes. At the rear of the pub is a small picnic area.

The opening hours are on Monday to Saturday from 12 noon to 2.30 pm and 7 pm to 11 pm, and on Sunday from 12 noon to 3 pm and 7 pm to 10.30 pm.

Telephone: 01780 410504.

How to get there: Turn off the A1 on the Stamford to Grantham section, on to the Castle Bytham signposted road, 10 miles north of Stamford or 3 miles south of the Colsterworth roundabout. Castle Bytham is 3½ miles off the main road, along the winding lane past Morkery Wood.

Parking: The inn does not have a car park, but there is some limited roadside parking outside the inn (for three or four cars) and in the immediate vicinity.

Length of the walk: 2¼ miles. Map: OS Landranger sheet 130 Grantham and surrounding area (inn GR 990184).

Castle Bytham is certainly one of the most interesting and scenic stone-built villages in the county. It is situated in a bowl and has all the attractions of a hillside village, plus a little stream flowing down to the river Glen. The huge, grassy earthworks are all that now remain of the once formidable castle. It was probably strengthened shortly after the Norman Conquest in 1066 by William the Conqueror's brother-in-law, Drogo. The Saxon owner of this bold site before the Conquest was Earl Morcar, whose name lives on in Morkery Wood to the west of the village.

This route, which can be shortened if your time is limited, is a pleasant, undemanding circuit, taking in the castle earthworks and even the remains of medieval fishponds.

The Walk

Turn up the signposted passage at the side of the Castle Inn, leading up to the church, and continue along the passage, with the stone wall on your right. At the end of the wall turn right up the tarmac path, with a wooden fence on your left, and walk on into the small estate.

Walk forward through Cumberland Gardens to turn right down to Morkery Lane. At the lane turn left downhill and, if you wish, you may shorten the walk by turning right down Water Lane, to rejoin the route at Castle Farm. Otherwise, climb for about 200 yards from Water Lane and there turn right off the road onto a signposted path. There are two public rights of way from this spot, but proceed diagonally right to a garden corner to follow the diverted path left to a stile and waymark (not as shown on the OS map). A second stile leads you into the village playing field, with two mounds on the left. Head directly right across the children's playground to the far right-hand corner

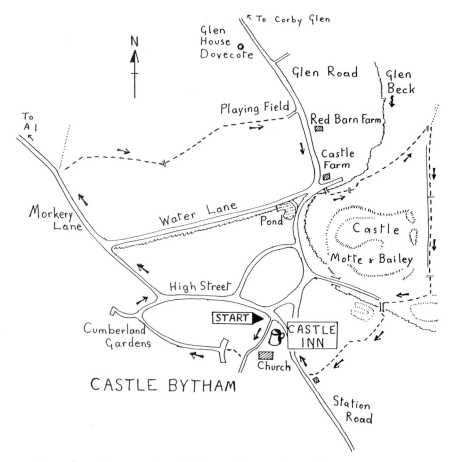

CASTLE BYTHAM

where there is a wooden fieldgate. On reaching the road turn right.

Proceed down the road for about 200 yards and at the end of the high wall of Castle Farm, cross the track to the signpost and footbridge over the stream. Go straight across the road here if you have walked down Water Lane.

Turn left after crossing the bridge, with the Castle Mound over on your right. Go over the paddock to a battered stile and then, ignoring the stile on your left, proceed uphill with a fence on your left until you reach the stile and ditchboard in the top left-hand corner of the field. Cross the footbridge to turn right, downhill, with the hedge on your right. Go over two more stiles and, upon reaching the attractive cricket pitch set in a bowl by the river, turn right to an awkward stile at the side of a metal fieldgate, labelled 'Castle Farm'.

It would be possible to proceed straight back into the village here.

Otherwise, turn left over the substantial metal footbridge across the infant river Glen. At the end of the bridge cross the stile and proceed uphill. The curious hollows on the right are the remains of medieval fishponds. Halfway up the hill go through the remnant hedge and continue uphill, with the hedge now on your left, until you reach the metal fieldgate leading into Station Road. The house on the left here was once the New Inn. Turn right, downhill, along Station Road into the High Street to return to the pub.

Other places of interest: Morkery Wood is Forestry Commission land. It has an extensive picnic site with rustic tables and you are free to wander at will.

4 Dyke
The Wishing Well

The Wishing Well is situated in the main street of this small hamlet, ½ mile off an old Roman road now known as the A15. The hamlet is called Dyke because it grew up on the west side of the Roman canal, the Car Dyke, which was an important means of communication in those times. In the past the hamlet was well served by public houses but today only one survives, the Crown, now renamed as the Wishing Well. Part of the inn appears to have been built in the 17th century but it is thought that it could be very much older. The large lounge bar is very attractive, with stone walling, beamed ceilings and pillars. Copper kitchen utensils decorate the walls and there are local paintings for sale. There is a games room with a dartboard and pool table. You can dine by candlelight in the two delightful restaurants, one large and one small. En suite accommodation is also available and outside you will find a pleasant children's play area with equipment.

Barry and Wendy Creaser will welcome you to this popular and picturesque freehouse, which gets its name from the original well to be found in the restaurant. Barry belongs to the Guild of Master Caterers, and the highly recommended cuisine certainly reflects his skill and interest. Food is served seven days a week, although the

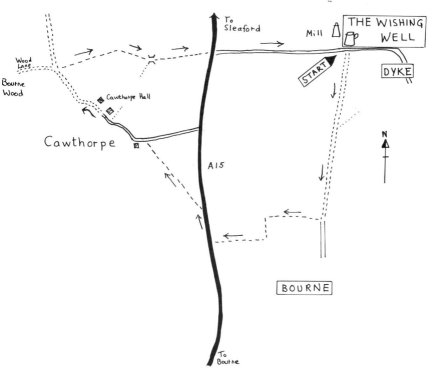

extensive bar menu is not available on Sundays and, on that day, it is essential to order your à la carte meal in advance. The standard menu includes unusual vegetarian dishes such as feuilletine, a pastry parcel filled with mushrooms in cheese and wine sauce, Veggie Special, or Spanish tortilla, salad, chips and peas. There is a wide choice of sandwiches and such culinary delights as home-made Guinness pie or cottage pie are just two of the items on offer. In warmer weather you can eat out of doors on the patio behind the inn. This is a freehouse, serving Draught Guinness, Carlsberg Export and Castlemaine Draught lagers, Copperhead and Symonds Scrumpy Jack ciders, Butcombe Bitter, Greene King Abbot Ale, Tetley Bitter, Ruddles County and normally one guest ale.

From Monday through to Saturday it is open from 11 am until 11 pm, and on Sunday from 12 noon to 3 pm and from 7 pm to 10.30 pm.

Telephone: 01778 422970.

How to get there: Turn off the A15 Bourne to Sleaford road 2 miles north of Bourne, where it is signposted 'Dyke'.

Parking: There is ample car parking space at the side of and behind the inn with, if necessary, alternative roadside parking in the immediate vicinity.

Length of the walk: 3 miles. Map: OS Landranger sheet 130 Grantham and surrounding area (inn GR 103225).

A pleasant walk in quiet countryside, mainly on good tracks and clearly defined footpaths, taking you within sight of Bourne Woods and by the old hall in the tiny hamlet of Cawthorpe.

The Walk

From the car park walk straight across the road to follow the sign-posted footpath along a good track. Continue along the track where it bends to the left, and then proceed straight forward for 800 yards.

Turn right off the track on to the signposted footpath with, at first, a dyke on your left and then turn left over the footbridge and imme-diately right, with the hedge and dyke now on your right, for 100 yards until the end of the field. Turn left along the field edge for another 100 yards and then right through the hedge, over the bridge and stile to the A15 road.

Turn right for 200 yards and then cross the road to take the clearly defined, signposted and stiled footpath diagonally right, across the field towards a modern house in Cawthorpe. The path leads into the garden and through the handgate on the left-hand side of the drive. Turn left into Cawthorpe to follow the lane round to the right past the old hall.

The lane becomes a track and at the T-junction with Wood Lane on the left, climb the bank on the right and follow the clear path over the crest of the slope to a waymark post at the edge of the next field. Walk straight forward to the stile and waymark. Cross the stile and go forward on the good track, with the hedge on the right, to the main road. Walk straight across the A15 and continue along the footway at the side of the lane, to the Wishing Well.

Pinchbeck
The Ship

Pinchbeck is a well-populated village and was a place of some importance in Saxon times, when it was attached to Crowland Abbey. Prosperity in the past came from flax and hemp but nowadays the parish covers thousands of acres of rich fenland, growing many different kinds of vegetables. At one time there were around 100 employees at the flax mill by the river bridge.

This picturesque, thatched, 400-year-old inn, in its riverside location, has a comfortable open-plan lounge bar, with attractive alcoves around the neat central bar servery, and is especially notable for its friendly, relaxed atmosphere. An extensive bar menu includes various sandwiches served with a choice of white, brown or French bread and salad. Chicken in coconut milk with ginger, stir-fry beef in oyster sauce and many more are all served with a choice of potato and two fresh vegetables. The main menu lists starters such as home-smoked duck breast with raspberry dressing, chef's seafood pancake, the Ship's special smokies, langoustine (4) in a black bean sauce or oriental chicken salad seasoned with burnt rice. Main courses can be freshly grilled mullet with oyster sauce, the Ship's mixed grill, sea trout in a fine lobster and cream sauce or the Ship's special chicken

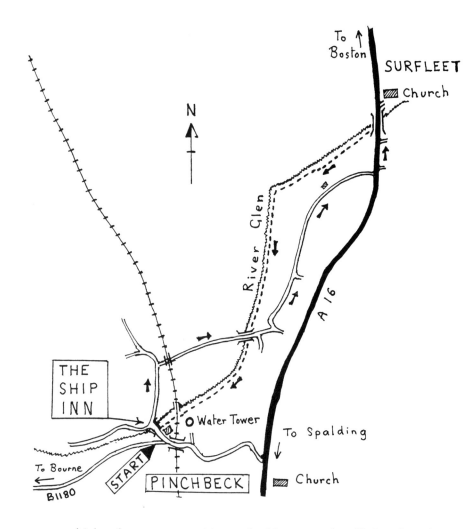

— a chicken breast wrapped in smoked bacon and stuffed with garlic butter prawns. In addition, a blackboard menu indicates the speciality of each day. There is also a Thai menu which must be ordered with at least 24 hours' notice.

This is a Courage house and the beers are Best Bitter, John Smith's Bitter, Chestnut Mild, Foster's Draught, with Draught Guinness, Taunton Dry Blackthorn cider and Kronenbourg 1664 lager. There is a large garden and a play area with equipment for children.

The inn is open on Monday to Friday from 12 noon to 2.30 pm and 7 pm to 11 pm, on Saturday from 12 noon to 4.30 pm and 6.30 pm to 11 pm, and on Sunday from 12 noon to 3 pm and 7 pm to 10.30 pm. Meals are served at lunchtime and in the evenings throughout the week.

Telephone: 01775 723792.

How to get there: Turn off the Boston–Stamford A16 road by the Bull Inn in Pinchbeck, 2½ miles north of Spalding, on to the B1180 Bourne Road. The Ship Inn is below the embankment on the right as you drive over the railway bridge, near the water tower.

Parking: There are ample parking places at the Ship, but if you are leaving a car while you are doing the walk please park away from the main entrance.

Length of the walk: 4 miles for the return walk to Surfleet, but the route can be reduced by turning back at the first bridge and walking along the river path. Map: OS Landranger sheet 131 Boston and surrounding area (inn GR 235260).

A walk, in an extraordinary backwater, towards Surfleet's curiously tilted church tower and spire at quite an alarming angle, along the little river Glen, near the end of its 30 mile journey to join the Welland, and by field upon field of vegetables of all kinds.

The Walk

From the inn car park turn left and walk up Northgate, over the river and almost immediately right up Herring Lane, with an unusual house on your right. After about 500 yards turn right up Langhole Drove to the railway crossing. Go over the crossing and walk forward for some 450 yards and over the river bridge.

For the shorter walk: Turn right to walk along the riverside path. Continue as in the final paragraph.

For the longer walk: Continue round to the left up Bacon's Lane. Go left at the junction, walking towards the leaning tower and spire of the church at Surfleet, along a narrow lane.

Turn left at the main road for 250 yards and, just past the general store and at the beginning of the footway for the road bridge, turn left over the stile, with the river Glen on your right. The footpath is sign-posted here 'Pinchbeck Station, 1¾ miles'. Follow this riverside path until you meet the bridge over the lane once again. Cross the bridge, with the river still on your right.

Continue along the riverside path until you reach the stile by the side of the water tower and another stile in order to cross the railway. The path then leads you directly into the car park of the Ship.

Other places of interest: Crowland, south of Spalding, with its unique triangular bridge at the junction of four streets where once three streams of the river Welland met. The Benedictine Abbey, founded in memory of King Ethelbald around the year 714, is still a spectacular building even though a partial ruin.

The Pinchbeck Engine, located on Pinchbeck Marsh, off West Marsh Road, Spalding. Built in 1833, with the coming of steam power, this enormous beam engine with an 18½ ft flywheel only ceased working in 1952. It may be seen from 10 am until 4 pm, April to October. There are also displays in the museum on land reclamation and conservation projects.

6 Gedney Drove End
The Rising Sun

The Rising Sun is probably named because it is set right on the edge of the East Coast and at times one may see beautiful sunrises across the marshes. There does not appear to have been any connection with smugglers although, at one time, there was quite a contraband trade with the Low Countries along this coast. A wide variety of customers have made the Rising Sun their own – members of the farming community throughout the year, aircraft enthusiasts observing spectacular NATO aircraft during their training on the adjacent bombing range, and wildfowlers and bird-watchers during the winter months from many walks of life and from all areas of the country.

After some 20 years in scientific instrument manufacturing and management David Osborne decided he would like a complete change in his way of life and he bought this small freehouse. There is always a warm and friendly welcome in this one-room country pub built in 1723. The attractive lounge bar with its walls covered with miscellaneous prints, foreign bank notes and assorted knick-knacks has bench seating, with an open fire whenever the weather merits one. Real ale is served as well as fresh bar snacks and a range of good-value plated meals. Rump steak, mushrooms, tomato and onion rings, for

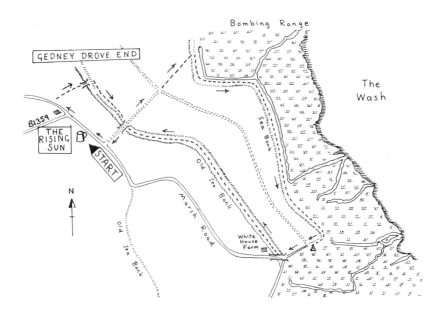

example, or home-cooked ham, egg and chips. The list of sandwiches includes steak in French bread, or prawns. The well-kept ales on handpump include Greene King Abbot, Greene King India Pale Ale and Bass. The draught lagers include Harp and Stella Artois. Well-behaved dogs are always welcome. Outside is a secluded beer garden and a play area for children. During the summer months, subject to fine weather, there are regular Sunday evening barbecues.

The pub opens at lunchtimes on Monday to Friday and Sunday from 12 noon to 3 pm, and on Saturday from 11 am to 4 pm. Evening opening is from 7 pm to 11 pm (10.30 pm on Sunday).

Telephone: 01406 550474.

How to get there: Turn off the A17 (T) King's Lynn to Sleaford road at Gedney on to the B1359. Gedney Drove End is 5½ miles along this road, via Gedney Dyke.

Parking: Customers may leave their cars in the Rising Sun car park, with the permission of the landlord, while they do the walk. Some roadside parking may be available within the village. Alternatively, there is a small car park on the verge by the trig point shown on the map at the seaward side of White House Farm and you could then walk towards the Rising Sun, with a stop for refreshment halfway through your walk.

Length of the walk: 3¼ miles. Map: OS Landranger sheet 131 Boston and surrounding area (inn GR 463293).

A walk with a difference along sea banks, old and new, with excellent bird-watching opportunities, especially during the winter months. The salt marshes have a unique flora because of the highly saline conditions and, where reclaimed, have become top quality arable land. Perhaps better at weekends, if you are not too keen on aircraft noise, for the planes do fly low over the area.

The Walk

Turn left out of the car park for 300 yards along the road and then turn right on the signposted footpath for 200 or so yards to a bridge and an old sea bank. Cross the bridge and turn right along the bank until you reach the lane. Turn left up the lane past the farm buildings and, on reaching the T-junction, walk straight forward on the signposted path to the sea. You should keep off the salt marshes themselves. The area can be dangerous without local knowledge as you may find yourself cut off when the tide comes in quickly. The creeks are deep and they are sometimes hidden.

Climb the sea bank and turn right to follow it round the various bends until you reach the bright orange marker used for indentification by aircraft practising on the bombing range. Turn right down the road towards White House Farm.

Leave the road to turn right along the Old Sea Bank just before the main road and continue, with the dyke on your left, until you reach your original lane. Turn left down the lane and right at the main road, back into the village and your starting place.

Harlaxton
The Gregory Arms

The Gregory Arms was originally an 18th century coaching inn on the road leading to Melton Mowbray and Gregory Gregory, the Lord of the Manor, granted the inn the favour of coal distribution throughout the area. At one time there was a wharf on the canal at Harlaxton Bridge. The pub itself is situated on the crossroads leading down into Harlaxton village but the view of Harlaxton Manor from the car park is not to be missed. The manor really is an incredible sight and over the years it has been used for a variety of purposes and also for the location of many films and television programmes. Locals in 'the Greg' have often been bemused by the characters and camera crews, providing them with much conversation and entertainment. The manor has had a chequered history, first as a stately home, then as a monastery and now the British campus of the University of Evansville, Indiana.

The Gregory Arms is a Scottish and Newcastle pub and Michael Kitt-Geraghty is the landlord. He makes everyone welcome not only in the bars but in the attractive Poachers Hyde restaurant. Real ales include Younger No. 3, Theakston XB, Younger's Draught Best Bitter and Home Bitter and Mild, with McEwan's lager, Guinness, Strongbow and

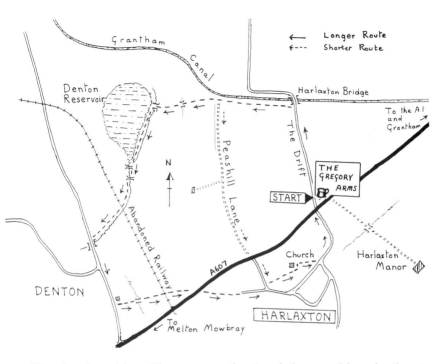

Woodpecker ciders. Blastaway – the Greg's long, cold cocktail – is featured on the notice board. Among the main course dishes are venison casserole, braised rabbit, trout with almonds and Poachers Hyde mixed grill. 'Specials' may be swordfish parcel or fresh salmon (poached or grilled). Vegetarian dishes are always available, such as cauliflower and leek au gratin served on a bed of pasta and covered in Stilton cheese sauce. A sensible note on the menu states 'Please note that good food takes time.' There are picnic tables in front of the pub and at the rear, away from the busy main road. A children's room is available and there is also a poolroom. Well-behaved dogs are welcome.

The pub is open on Monday to Saturday from 11 am to 2.30 pm and 6 pm to 11 pm, and on Sunday from 12 noon to 3 pm and 7 pm to 10.30 pm. No food is served on Sunday and Monday evenings.

Telephone: 01476 564587.

How to get there: Turn off the A1 (the Great North Road) south of Grantham onto the A607 Melton Mowbray road and continue for 1 mile to Harlaxton crossroads.

Parking: There is a very large car park belonging to the pub. Alternative parking may be available on the wide grass verge of The Drift.

Length of the walk: 2 miles or 3¼ miles for the much more interesting route. Map: OS Landranger sheet 130 Grantham and surrounding area (inn GR 884331).

A most pleasant walk by a tranquil disused canal and along the banks of an attractive canal reservoir, teeming with bird life.

The Walk

Turn right out of the car park and almost immediately right again down The Drift. After 900 yards, and just before reaching Harlaxton Bridge over the canal, turn left up the steps to the stile on the signposted footpath and walk across the grass field, with the canal on your right.

For the shorter walk: At the wide gap in the hedge, where the canal turns right, turn left towards the farmhouse, with a hedge on your right. This is Peashill Lane, although only a grass track at first. Follow this lane up to the main road and then cross to the lane leading into Harlaxton village directly opposite. When you reach the signposted path on the left by the lane junction you are rejoining the longer route (see final paragraph).

For the longer walk: At the wide gap in the hedge bear left across the paddock, with the hedge on your immediate left, until you reach the footbridge with stiles at each end. After crossing the bridge, climb the steps to the banks of Denton Reservoir and turn left. Follow this wide track over the concrete bridge above the weir and continue forward at the first bridge on the right. At the second footbridge turn right and then left, with the stream now on your left. Climb the stile and cross the line of the old mineral railway and continue forward to the lane. It is often muddy on this stretch because of cattle.

At the lane turn left into Denton village. Walk straight forward at the road junction, and 300 yards beyond it, turn left on the signposted path just past the red telephone box situated in the garden of the post office. Climb the stile and walk towards the spire of Harlaxton church and, on descending into the valley, you will discover a bridge with a white painted handrail over the stream. Walk up the field on the defined path to the main road. Cross the road and proceed diagonally left on the signposted path. In the corner by the stone wall you will find a stile leading you into the small lane called West End.

At the lane junction take the signposted footpath through the kissing-gate leading you to the church. Walk on past the front of the church to take the first metalled path behind the church leading to the right and not the path proceeding straight to the cottage. At the end of your path go down the stone steps into Church Street and turn left along the High Street to the crossroads, with a number of interesting houses to be seen en route.

Other places of interest: Harlaxton Manor Gardens are open daily for visitors from April until October betwen 11 am and 5 pm, except on Mondays. However, they are also open on bank holidays, including Mondays.

8 Old Somerby
The Fox and Hounds

The converted 19th century farmhouse, known today as the Fox and Hounds, is situated in the lovely hamlet of Old Somerby. Here Tony and Karen Cawthorn have created a splendid establishment, offering food of real excellence. The menu states that they have one aim, 'to make your visit to our pub as pleasant and relaxing as possible' and I would add the word 'memorable'.

The dining-room has its own comprehensive menu specialising in seafood and steaks. Calamari (squid) grilled and served with parsley and garlic butter, poached plaice in a sauce of prawns, cockles, mussels, scallops, white wine and fresh cream, fresh crab 'au gratin', battered jumbo scampi, peppered steak pan-fried in a cream sauce and sirloin à la crème with onions, mushrooms, brandy and cream are just some of the items on the restaurant menu. It promises that no artificial flavourings are used – 'Our steaks are served undiluted'. The range of food served in both the restaurant and bar is quite staggering. The set menus are also supplemented by a range of home-made speciality dishes, announced daily on the blackboards displayed in the bar, for example, pan-fried duck breast with blackcurrants, vegetable tortilla or marinated herring salad. In addition, Tony's award-winning

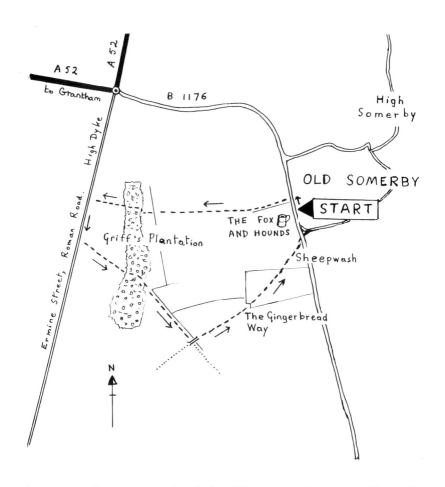

'submarines' – hot roast beef plus filling in a roll – are well worthy of consideration for a quick bar meal. There are also numerous desserts. This is a traditional freehouse serving an equally wide range of real ales, including Webster's Yorkshire Bitter, Ruddles County, Marston's Pedigree and Owd Rodger, plus Carlsberg and Kronenbourg lagers, Scrumpy Jack cider and draught Beamish. There is a large beer garden with a number of tables and a children's area. Dogs are not permitted indoors.

The pub is open from 11 am to 2.30 pm and 7 pm to 11 pm from Tuesday to Saturday and on Sundays from 12 noon to 3 pm and 7 pm to 10.30 pm. It always closes on Mondays.

Telephone: 01476 64121.

How to get there: At the roundabout 3 miles east of Grantham on the A52 Grantham to Boston road, take the B1176 road for 1 mile to Old Somerby.

Parking: There is a large car park, with an overflow on the other side of the pub.

Length of the walk: 2 ¼ miles. Map: OS Landranger sheet 130 Grantham and surrounding area (inn GR 955334).

An undramatic but pleasant walk across a number of grassy fields, along hedgerows and through a small plantation. Some of the field corners will be muddy in wet weather and it would be wise to have stout footwear.

The Walk

Turn left out of the pub car park and, within a few yards, left over a stile on a signposted path. Keep to the left edge of the field to a stile in the far corner. Walk across the next grass field towards Griff's Plantation, aiming for the prominent tree in the field hedge in front of the wood and a wooden fieldgate, when it comes into view. Go through this gate and keep to the edge of the field until you reach the wood, and then proceed along the outside until you reach a pleasant green track through the wood about 70 yards from the field corner. Walk along this grassy ride and then along the hedge on your left until you reach the Ermine Street Roman road.

Turn left for 350 yards and then left again into the field on the signposted path, with the hedge on your immediate left, until you again reach the wood. Enter the wood on the cleared path and then take the headland path, with the hedge on your left. Be careful here to follow the correct hedgeline. Continue along this headland for 900 yards until you reach a footbridge and various waymarks, for this is part of The Gingerbread Way, a recreational route around Grantham. Turn left over the footbridge and then diagonally left across the field on a clear path towards a gap in the hedge, a wooden fieldgate and a concealed stile in the field edge. Go diagonally left again across another grass field to a metal gate with a stile in the hedge. After crossing the stile keep to the right-hand edge of the field with a large pond (Sheepwash) on your right over the hedge. Cross a stile and bear slightly left to the gate, stile and signpost at Low Somerby and The Pastures T-junction. Turn left down Grantham Road to the Fox and Hounds.

9 Newton
The Red Lion

Graham Watkin is the landlord of this attractive freehouse in a picturesque and secluded village off the main Boston to Grantham road. The road itself is old, being an ancient saltway from the saltpans on the coast to the tribes of Middle England. There was a settlement and a church recorded here in the Domesday Book in 1086 and in the 8th century an alehouse probably stood on the site of the present Red Lion. It is a common name for a very uncommon pub – there cannot be many that double as a butcher's and a bakery. Graham was formerly a pork butcher and he clearly has not lost his skill for he still stuffs chine, roasts beef ribs and makes his own sausages. The smell of bread, cakes and sausage rolls pervades the early morning air as he delivers to a shop in Grantham ready for an 8.30 am opening.

There are some lovely footpaths hereabouts but they all seem to lead to the Red Lion where friendly, personal attention is in constant supply. The building itself is obviously fairly old, with its mellow Lincolnshire stone and wistaria draping along its walls. One large bar has several serving rooms leading from it and an old world atmosphere is much in evidence. Cushioned settles, exposed stone in places and the quarry tiled floor reflect the pub's 17th century origins and the walls are lined with sporting cartoons, wheels and farm artefacts. There is a very pleasant sheltered outdoor play area with equipment

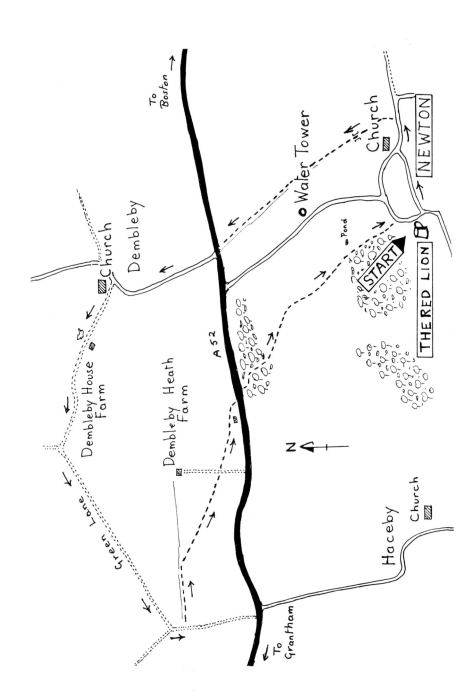

To Boston →

To Grantham

42

and well-behaved children are welcome anywhere in the pub. Dogs are not permitted in the bar or the garden area where children play. In a separate wing there are two squash courts and whirlpool baths that are open to the public at weekends. There are also six rooms in self-contained cottages, all en suite, under separate management, offering remarkably good value for bed and breakfast arrangements.

The menu changes daily, depending upon what is in the market place or in season. The cold carvery is renowned and you may find as many options as pâté, prawns, mackerel, ox tongue, pork, beef, home-cured ham and turkey. The home-made soups and puddings are also much in demand. There is also a hot carvery with dishes like the carbonade of beef. On Friday and Saturday evenings, as well as Sunday lunchtimes, there is a choice of roast. A real ale pub, on tap are Bateman, Bass and John Smith's. Lagers are Tennents, Stella Artois and Carlsberg. Draught Guinness is available and also Swanlight low alcohol.

The pub is open each lunchtime from 11.30 am to 3 pm and in the evenings from 6 pm to 11 pm (7 pm to 10.30 pm on Sundays). Food may be ordered from 12 noon until 2 pm and from 7 pm until 10.10 pm and it is wise to book a meal in advance from Friday onwards.

Telephone: 01529 497256.

How to get there: Newton village is 1 mile south of the A52 Boston to Grantham road, 2 miles west of Threekingham roundabout, and 10 miles east of Grantham.

Parking: Customers may leave their cars in front of the Red Lion while they are doing the walk. Limited alternative parking is available within the village limits, although some roadside parking may be possible opposite the church, near the old school – with care, for large farm machinery uses the road.

Length of the walk: 4½ miles. Map: OS Landranger sheet 130 Grantham and surrounding area (inn GR 045361).

Sixpenny Hill at Newton is so called because in the 18th century there was a toll bar closing off the turnpike road that is now the A52. It is said that from here there is nothing higher between you and the Ural Mountains in Russia. There has been woodland behind the Red Lion for hundreds of years and the mature trees and dense cover provide shelter for the feral herds of fallow deer which may be seen throughout the area of the walk. During the summer months you may hear a woodpecker or see a sparrowhawk searching the hedgerows. The last part of your walk brings you along the edge of this private woodland.

The Walk

Turn right out of the pub and then left along the lane at the T-junction, past the old school on the right and then the church on your left. About 200 yards beyond the church turn left off the lane on the signposted path, to walk down into the valley and then across the footbridge. Continue straight forward up the other side of the valley, with the water tower over on your left. Proceed downhill to the road, with the small dyke on your immediate left.

Cross the busy main road and walk up the quiet lane towards Dembleby. At the bend in the road by Dembleby church turn left towards Dembleby House Farm, with a pond below you on the right. Continue foward along this little lane that soon becomes a track after the farm, and avoid turning right on to another clear farm track. Dembleby Thorns Wood can be seen over on your right and the track now becomes a real green lane.

About ¾ mile beyond Dembleby House Farm turn left at a wide green track junction (signposted) for 100 yards and then left again, with the hedge on your left. After 300 yards (waymark), head diagonally right across the field on the clearly defined footpath and, after crossing the track leading to Dembleby Heath Farm, aim just to the left of the wooded quarry now occupied by a kennels. Walk down the slope to the road and cross to the other side where a footpath signpost stands at the entrance to a fieldgate. Walk up the slope to the edge of the thicket and make your way through the Stonepit Plantation. Walk across the arable field down into the valley and cross the dyke, to climb steeply uphill to the right-hand edge of the field. Walk to the left around the edge of the wood, with a small pond on your left, and then by an overgrown, wooden fieldgate straight across the paddock to the Red Lion.

Aswarby
The Tally Ho Inn

A welcoming stone-built 17th century inn that has been a hostelry and coach stop on the Bourne–Sleaford road for over 100 years. It is situated among gentle, rolling wooded countryside on a bend in the road, looking across the field to where Aswarby church and a few grey stone cottages remain at the entrance to the hall grounds, but the village itself was removed by order of the squire and the great house, long the home of the Whichcotes, was destroyed by a disastrous fire and pulled down in 1947.

William Wood has made many changes to this freehouse, refurbishing the restaurant and converting the stables and dairy into six very pleasant en suite bedrooms. Lots of comfortable seating, old beams and a stone fireplace with log fires in winter make the lounge bar snug and cosy. Hunting pictures on the walls and a map showing fox and staghound packs throughout the United Kingdom relate to its hunting connections, for the Belvoir Hunt meets here on the paddock behind the inn. The aim is to provide higher than expected standards of cooking and plenty of choice and originality, along with friendly, informal service. Bar meals are certainly different, for they include dishes such as Mexican chicken (grilled chicken drumsticks marinated

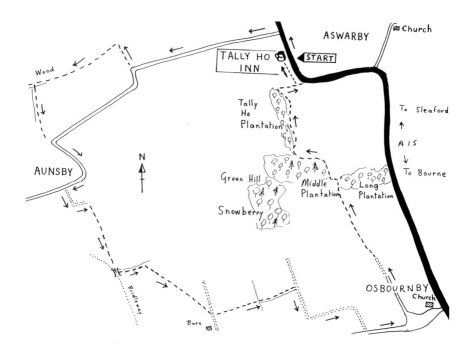

in chillies, coriander and yoghurt), poached salmon salad, gratin of courgettes and pasta, braised beef in ale, sizzling ribs or spinach and pepper quiche, as well as ploughman's lunches. The restaurant menu is recognised as being one of the finest in the area, with starters such as hot devilled crab pot, cold charcuterie, warm duck salad or Stilton, port and celery mousse. Main course dishes range from rabbit casseroled with mustard and wine, country chicken casserole cooked in sherry with vegetables and fresh herbs to hot poached salmon with a watercress, wine and cream sauce, and there is a variety of splendid desserts. Meals are served at lunchtime and in the evening throughout the week. Fine draught ales are served, Bateman, Abbot and Bass, plus guest ales from time to time. Stella and Carling lagers and Scrumpy Jack cider are also available. Children are welcome and there is a play area in the garden. Picnic tables are scattered around the lawn behind the inn for warmer days. Well-behaved dogs are permitted.

The inn is open from 12 noon to 2.30 pm at lunchtime and from 6.30 pm to 10 pm every evening (7 pm on Sunday).

Telephone: 01529 455205.

How to get there: The inn is situated on the A15 Sleaford to Bourne road some 4 miles south of the Sleaford bypass roundabout or 13 miles north of Bourne.

Parking: There is some parking in front of the inn, with additional parking behind. It is only courteous, though, to inform the landlord if you intend to leave your car when you want to do the walk, and then to park in one of the remote corners of the car park rather than by the front door.

Length of the walk: 4½ miles. Map: OS Landranger sheet 130 Grantham and surrounding area (inn GR 061395).

An undemanding walk that explores level footpaths, bridleways and lanes. There is only one, moderate, hill yet the route offers attractive, unexpected views over wooded countryside, enormous fields and distant villages with intriguing names like Scott Willoughby. Indeed, some sections of the walk seem surprisingly remote despite the proximity of an A road.

The Walk

From the inn turn left along the main road towards Sleaford for 200 yards and then left again up the quiet lane leading to Aunsby. At the first left-hand bend in the road, turn right on a waymarked, signposted bridleway. Turn left at the first hedge, with the hedge and ditch on your immediate left. Halfway along the wood on the right, turn left across the ditch and proceed forward with a ditch on your right until you reach the lane leading into Aunsby.

At the lane walk straight forward into the village and, just round the bend by the council houses, turn left through a metal fieldgate to follow the track on the signposted, diverted bridleway. Bear left on the track and go through the second metal fieldgate to turn right, uphill, along the line of trees on your right. Continue forward past the electricity pylon to the bridleway bridge. You have a choice here.

The bridleway continues straight forward down the slope to the road and then you turn left along the lane to Osbournby.

For the alternative route, after crossing the bridge, continue on the footpath along the edge of the dyke on the left for 300 yards and then bear diagonally right across the field to a point on the track leading up from the abandoned farm buildings near the road. Cross the farm track (waymark) and go forward over the field to proceed towards the field corner. Cross the ditch and continue forward with a hedge now on your right and, upon reaching the farm track, follow it round to your right and the lane. Turn left.

Upon reaching Osbournby's extraordinarily wide village square, turn left up North Street. At the end of the metalled lane continue uphill along the wide, grass track with the hedge on your left. There is a seat at the top of the hill for you to rest and enjoy the view, with Long Plantation on your right and an ancient kissing-gate.

Go through the gate to bear left along the field edge, skirting Middle Plantation and Tally Ho Plantation. On reaching the stream (waymark) turn right with the dyke on your left until you reach the little copse and a signpost on the main road. Then turn left for a few yards round the bend in the road to the Tally Ho Inn. However, by arrangement of the landlord, to avoid the dangerous road bend, go through the wooden fieldgate just by the roadside copse and across the paddock to the inn, where you will find a stile in the fence which leads you into the car park.

Anton's Gowt
The Oak Tree

Peter and Margaret Parkin are the proprietors of this fine Victorian inn, which has been considerably extended and tastefully modernised. It was formerly called the Malcolm Arms. There is a splendid conservatory dining-room that is a lovely, light place to eat, overlooking the garden. In summertime the Oak Tree is a haunt for both anglers and boating enthusiasts from the nearby river Witham. Peter and his son Mark are brave men for, in January 1994, they dived into the swollen, icy waters of the Frith Drain and successfully rescued a woman and her two children, aged three and five years, after her car had skidded off the road on black ice by the bridge.

The bar food is listed on an incredible 46-selection bar meal menu, including a large range of cold meat and fish salads. The restaurant menu has 52 different dishes, and the Sunday lunch is outstanding value with a choice of six starters, four main courses, a sweet trolley carrying ten choices, plus coffee and a mint. There are also 13 vegetarian meals and a separate children's menu. Well-kept Bateman, Tetley and Marston's Pedigree beers are on handpump, and there is Draught Guinness as well as lagers and ciders. This is a freehouse with a no-smoking area, an outside patio, a family room, a games room and

49

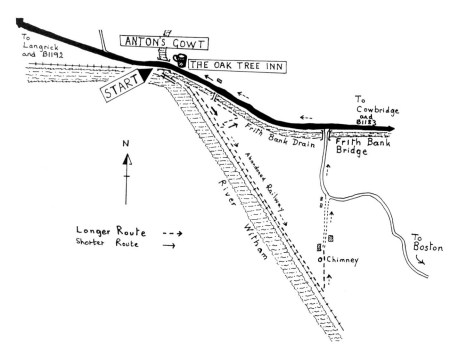

a garden for children. There are also facilities for disabled/wheelchair entry to the pub. Dogs are not permitted in the inn.

The inn is open each day from 12 noon to 2.30 pm (3 pm on Sunday), and in the evening from 7 pm to 11 pm (opening at 6.30 pm on Saturday). It is wise to book in advance for a meal at weekends. Telephone: 01205 360369.

How to get there: Turn off the A1121 Swineshead Bridge to Boston road at Hubbert's Bridge. Continue to Langrick and then Anton's Gowt Lane is signposted in the hamlet. Alternatively, from the B1183 Boston to Horncastle road, turn off to Anton's Gowt at Cowbridge.

Parking: Customers may leave their cars in the very large car park at the Oak Tree while they are doing the walk, but do please park away from the main entrance. There is limited off-road parking by the road bridge at the side of the lock gates.

Length of the walk: 3 miles or a short walk of ¾ mile. Map: OS Land-ranger sheet 131 Boston and surrounding area (inn GR 301475).

50

The word 'gowt' means a sluice but the more common name locally is Anton's Gowt Lock. This is a waterside walk with a river, wide drains and lakes, all supporting plenty of bird life and there is a good chance of seeing deer in the small nature reserve opposite the Oak Tree. St Botolph's magnificent lantern tower, rising 272½ ft, has been a guide to travellers by land and sea for centuries. It was completed in 1460 although the foundations were begun in 1309. You walk towards it for part of each walk and seen from afar you can decide for yourself whether it merits the local name of Boston Stump.

The Walk

Turn right out of the car park for a few yards to the road bridge on the bend and then go left on the signposted path, with the lock gates on your left. Cross the line of the old railway to turn left over the lock gate with the broad river Witham on your right and the lock-keeper's cottage and his extensive garden on the left. Walk forward along the river bank for about 350 yards, with the abandoned railway beside you and Boston Stump directly ahead.

For the shorter walk: Turn left off the riverside path through an iron handgate, cross the line of the old railway and follow the waymarked path round the line of the newly extended nature reserve. This public footpath has been diverted and the new route may not be shown on OS maps. It is a good wide path with newly planted trees on the left. At the end of the deer paddock turn left towards Frith Drain and left again on reaching the drain and continue as far as the large wooden bridge. Cross the bridge and turn left up the road with the modern Holland House on your right and the lakes of the nature reserve across the drain on your left. Deer may often be seen sheltering in the trees by the lakes. The Oak Tree is a few yards up the road.

For the longer walk: Continue along the river bank for another mile and turn left off it at the three-fingered metal signpost situated opposite the industrial chimney. The public footpath actually goes through the building complex of the old station yard and by the foot of the chimney, but generations of local people have avoided doing so by walking down the far better track on the opposite side of the hedge, that is, keeping the hedgeline and ditch on your immediate left until you reach the lane, where, in fact, the path is signposted showing this route. Walk up to the lane junction and turn left opposite the newly built thatched house and around the road bends for ½ mile until you reach the bridge over the Frith Drain. Go over this bridge and turn left back to the Oak Tree.

⑫ Coleby
The Bell Inn

The Bell is a delightful, low-beamed pub with real character, situated in Far Lane, directly behind the church, which has a light on its crocketed spire to warn aircraft landing at the nearby Waddington airfield. It has always been an unofficial officers' mess for flying crews from Waddington and Swinderby and, even today, you may well find aircrews from France, Germany, the United States or even Russia in the bar. The American car number plates from different states on the beams are quite a change from horse brasses. There is a very pleasant black-beamed dining area with cushioned settles and a series of nooks, a main lounge bar with a huge barrel-shaped fireplace and an open fire in winter, and also an upper lounge with its own open fireplace. There is also a poolroom.

The pub offers well-kept Marston's Bitter, Ansells Bitter, Tetley Bitter and Marston's Pedigree Bitter, with customers coming for cask rather than keg beers. Lagers include Labatt's Canadian, Stella Artois and Castlemaine. Murphy's Irish Stout and Dry Blackthorn cider complete the range of drinks available. Examples of the extensive bar menu described on the blackboard are a bowl of hot chilli with granary bread, burgers or Lincolnshire sausage and chips. Main course meals include beef steak, mushrooms and Guinness, chicken en croûte (chicken breast, smoked salmon and prawns, in puff pastry, with a cream and mushroom sauce), swordfish steak pan fried in garlic butter or rack of lamb with red wine. Tasty, home-cooked vegetarian dishes are also available, such as cauliflower and broccoli florets mixed with onions, in a rich cheese sauce with walnuts, or mushroooms and tagliatelle in a chilli sauce.

The Bell is open on Monday to Saturday from 11 am to 3 pm and 7 pm to 11 pm, and on Sunday from 12 noon to 3 pm and 7 pm to 10.30 pm. Meals are served from 12 noon to 2 pm and from 7 pm to 10 pm.

Telephone: 01522 810240.

How to get there: Coleby is signposted off the A607 Lincoln to Grantham road between Harmston and Boothby Graffoe, some 7 miles south of Lincoln.

Parking: Customers may park in the pub car park while they are doing the walk. Alternatively, there may be roadside parking at the side of the village green triangle at the bottom of High Street, opposite the Tempest Arms.

Length of the walk: 2½ miles. Map: OS Landranger sheet 121 Lincoln and surrounding area (inn GR 976607).

The walk takes in one of the most attractive parts of the Viking Way long distance recreational path, where this section along the narrow western ridge, called 'The Cliff', joins a string of stone-built, spring-line villages with extensive views over the Witham valley and onwards to the river Trent and Nottinghamshire.

The Walk
Turn left out of the car park to the end of Far Lane. There is a half-concealed stile on the left of the metal fieldgate. Climb this stile to turn left off the path after only a few yards, at the third stile leading you into Church Lane. Walk up the lane, with the church on your left, and turn right at the road junction to walk down High Street. At the bottom, walk across the triangle of the village green, with the Tempest Arms on your right.

Turn left up the narrow, signposted path with a Viking Way waymark, with No 3 Hill Rise on your right, and continue on this well-marked path along the cliff edge for about ¾ mile until you near Boothby Graffoe.

Turn left (waymark) over the stile by the metal fieldgate on your left and walk diagonally across the grass paddock to the gate and stile in

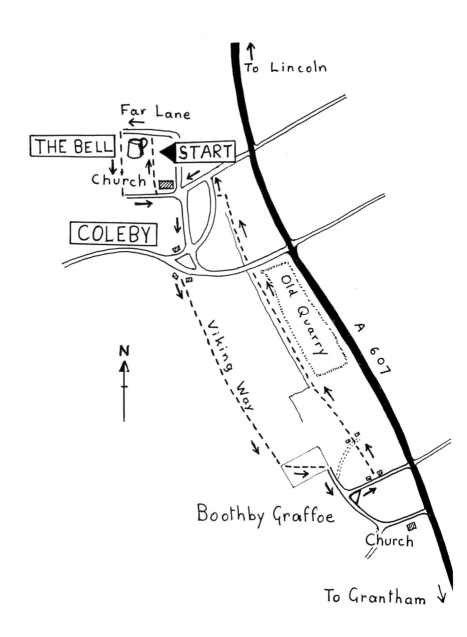

To Lincoln

Far Lane

THE BELL START

Church

COLEBY

Old Quarry

A 607

N

Viking Way

Boothby Graffoe

Church

To Grantham ↓

the right-hand corner of the field. Walk down Far End Lane, with the Keeper's Cottage, and often a painted gypsy caravan, on the right. At the road junction with Main Street, turn left, uphill, with the attractive little green public enclosure called Henson's Lawn on your right. It is a good place for an apple stop.

After about 150 yards turn left up four concrete steps on to a sign-posted footpath with a stile and continue along the narrow pathway until the end of the garden, to a gate and stile. Cross the small paddock to a step stile with the fence on your immediate right. Go over the farm track to walk between the two farm buildings (waymark), then through the metal fieldgate to go straight forward across the arable field, walking directly towards Coleby church spire. At the hedge corner you will meet a track. Continue along this until you meet the lane leading into Coleby. Cross this lane and continue straight forward, with the stone wall on your left, to a stile. At the next stile turn left down the alleyway (this path has been diverted and may not be as shown on the OS map) and on into Blind Lane. Turn right, with the school on your left, and then left towards the church. Walk up Church Lane to turn right up the path leading to the church, which is well worth a visit, and follow this round through the graveyard, on to Far Lane and your starting place.

13 Tattershall Thorpe
The Blue Bell

This beautiful old building dates back to 1257 and is documented as being an inn since the 16th century. It has its own priest's hole and, it is said, a resident ghost. During the Second World War, the pub became a favourite off-base rendezvous for officers and men from the nearby airfields and it is full of photographs and memorabilia, such as a flight log-sheet of a run-up to the Dambusters raid, photographs of Wing Commander Guy Gibson receiving his VC at Buckingham Palace, 627 Pathfinder Squadron flying Mosquitoes, Lancasters from 97 Squadron, 619 Squadron and men of the 617 (Dambusters) Squadron celebrating the sinking of the Tirpitz. An old propeller blade stands guard at the entrance.

The present owners, Eric and Joan Johnson, have succeeded in creating a friendly hostelry with an enviable reputation. The delightful, cosy, low-beamed lounge bar has an attractive inglenook with an open fire. The extensive bar menu caters for all tastes and includes various sandwiches, baked potatoes with a range of fillings, 'steakwich', chip butty and ploughman's. Among items served for starters are soup, garlic mushrooms, giant prawns in garlic, chicken goujon with dip, whitebait, prawn cocktail and 'wings of fire'. Main courses include haddock, chips and peas, chicken tikka with nan and pilau rice, lasagne Romano, chips and garlic bread, chicken, ham and leek pie, lamb Madras and fillet steak. There is also a house speciality of a seven-meat mixed grill. Sweets range from toffee apple and pecan pie, treacle sponge and custard, to hot chocolate fudge cake and death by chocolate. This is a freehouse and there are well-kept, hand-pumped John Smith's Bitter and Marston's Pedigree plus two guest ales that are changed at frequent intervals. Draught Guinness, Scrumpy Jack cider, and Foster's and Beck's lagers are also available. There is a poolroom (mind your head) with dartboard and a snug little 20-seater separate restaurant. In warm weather meals and drinks can be enjoyed in the peaceful surrounds of the old orchard, while the seven acres attached to the inn allow children to play in safety away from the road.

The inn is open from Monday to Saturday from 12 noon to 2.30 pm and 7 pm to 11 pm. On Sundays it is open from 12 noon to 3 pm but closed in the evening. During the summer months the opening hours may be extended.

Telephone: 01526 342206.

How to get there: Tattershall Thorpe is on the B1192, Woodhall Spa to Coningsby road, about 1 mile from the A153 at Coningsby Bridge.

Parking: Park in the large car park of the inn or, alternatively, roadside parking may be possible in the small lay-by by the telephone kiosk a couple of hundred yards down Thorpe Road.

Length of the walk: 1 ¾ miles, which could be extended by walking further round the perimeter path of either wood. Map: OS Landranger sheet 122 Skegness area (inn GR 219594).

A delightful walk through mature deciduous woodland, mainly of firm paths, in an area of intensively cultivated agricultural land in the Bain valley. During the walk there is evidence of the part Lincolnshire played as Bomber County during the Second World War.

Tattershall Thorpe itself is a hamlet standing near the old river Bain and the Horncastle Canal with numerous old flooded gravel pits in the vicinity that have become attractive to many bird species and a mecca for bird-watchers. Nearby Tattershall Castle, begun in 1230 and now owned by the National Trust, dominates the surrounding countryside.

The Walk

From the pub car park cross the road to the footway and turn left past the Wesleyan chapel on the left. Re-cross the road to turn into the tarmac entrance to the old RAF camp, at present being rehabilitated as

57

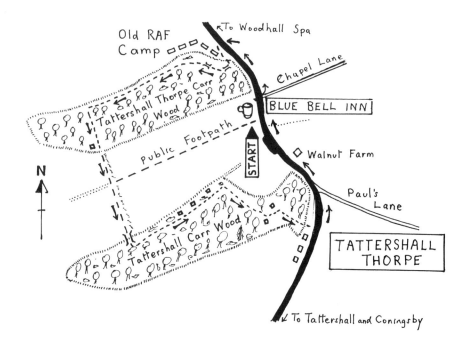

an example of a wartime camp for a bomber base. After a few yards turn left parallel to the road for a hundred yards and then right on the concrete track towards the wood. Cross the stout ditchboard with the Woodland Trust sign nearby. Turn right over the second wooden footbridge to follow the good path along the wood edge. Turn left at a clear path junction, go over the stream and, at the other edge of the wood, you will see a bomb-blast shelter on your right.

Walk straight forward along the newly created path joining the two sections of woodland. There are newly planted trees on your left and right. If you need to shorten your walk, at the track crossroads simply turn left back to the road and the pub, otherwise continue straight forward to Tattershall Carr Wood. Cross the wide wooden bridge and turn left along the wood edge with air-raid shelters and bomb-blast shelters on your left. Do not go through the metal fieldgate but continue along the perimeter path to the right, to take the first clear track to the left past another bomb-blast shelter, still on your left. The path takes you to the road and a locked, wooden fieldgate, but there is a pedestrian access gap on the right of the gate. Cross the road and turn left along the footway around the bend until you are opposite the pub, and then re-cross the road again to your starting place.

Other places of interest: The pine woods at Woodhall Spa belonging to the Woodland Trust, and Tattershall Castle owned by the National Trust. The present castle dates from around 1440 and was built for Ralph Cromwell, treasurer of England. It is an important example of early brick building, and both Lincoln Cathedral and Boston Stump may be seen from its tower on clear days. Picnicking is welcome in the grounds.

14 Southrey
The Riverside Inn

The inn is about 100 years old and once served the chain ferry across the river Witham. There was formerly a railway station nearby, on the Wragby to Woodhall Spa line, but it fell to the Beeching axe. The inn has been renamed more than once but the most recent, the Riverside Inn, seems much more appropriate than Faulty Towers. It is a family-run freehouse with Brian and Lynn Walley as the landlords. Lynn, with a background in catering has brought her knowledge and skills to the Riverside and she intends to maintain the well-established excellent reputation for good-quality, home-cooked food, using local produce wherever possible. It is a popular fisherman's pub during the season and a well-used local throughout the year. Outside is a beer garden and a play area for children. Inside, there is an open fireplace in the lounge bar and a pool table in the bar alcove. Well-behaved dogs are welcome.

A sample of the food on offer is whitebait, prawn and chicken curry with poppadums and chutney, duck with peaches and brandy and turkey cordon bleu. A blackboard menu lists the sweets available, such as treacle and walnut tart and coffee and mandarin gateau, and the special dish of the day. Wholesome bar snacks and jacket potatoes

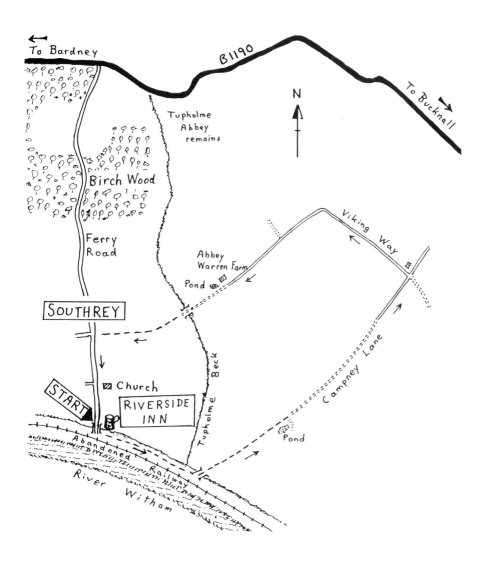

To Bardney

B1190

To Bucknall

N

Tupholme
Abbey
remains

Birch Wood

Viking Way

Ferry
Road

Abbey
Warren Farm

Pond

SOUTHREY

Tupholme Beck

Campney Lane

Church

START

RIVERSIDE
INN

Pond

Abandoned   Railway

River   Witham

with various fillings are always available. No food is served on Mondays otherwise the full menu is available at all times, with the exception of Sunday lunchtime when there is the traditional set roast lunch. There is a children's menu for youngsters twelve years of age and under. Draught Guinness, Scrumpy Jack and Woodpecker ciders are available. The range of beer on handpump includes Bateman and Bass and Foster's Draught, and a guest ale, such as Young's Winter Warmer. Kaliber alcohol-free lager is also available.

The inn is open on Monday to Saturday from 12 noon to 2 pm and 7 pm to 11 pm and on Sunday from 12 noon to 3 pm and 7 pm to 10.30 pm.

Telephone: 01526 398374.

How to get there: Turn off the B1190 Bardney to Horncastle road on the signposted Southrey cul-de-sac, 1 ½ miles after Bardney or 3 miles after Bucknall.

Parking: Customers may leave their cars in the inn car park while they are doing the walk. Alternative roadside parking is available along Ferry Road.

Length of the walk: 3 ¼ miles. Map: OS Landranger sheet 121 Lincoln and surrounding area (inn GR 138665).

Wide horizon country in the flatlands of the Witham valley. An easy stroll at the end of a pleasant wooded road that once led to a river crossing. There are distant views of the Lincolnshire Wolds and nearby, the ruins of Tupholme Abbey and Forestry Commission woods.

The Walk

Turn right out of the inn car park towards the river Witham and then left along the railway track past the former Southrey station platform. The signposted path is down by the beck on the left but generations of walkers have used the firmer track of the old railbed well above the river.

After about 900 yards, turn left down the embankment to cross the stout footbridge with handrails and then follow the good track that eventually becomes the green lane called Campney Lane. Follow this lane for about a mile and, at the track crossroads, turn left to join a section of The Viking Way long-distance recreational path. This metalled track leads you to Abbey Warren Farm where you walk forward, with a large pond on your immediate right. Continue straight forward though the wooden fieldgate and proceed to the bridge over Tupholme Beck and then on to Ferry Road.

Turn left at the road to pass the wooden, clapboard 'New England' type church with its attractive wind vane, and continue to the Riverside Inn.

Other places of interest: The nearby Tupholme Abbey ruins are set in a wildlife conservation area with picnic tables and a visual display board offering a short, illustrated history of Tupholme.

Nearby Bardney has the ruins of a 7th century abbey, the resting place of King Ethelred of Mercia. The abbey was destroyed by Henry VIII in 1538.

15 Dunholme
The Four Seasons

The Four Seasons is a modern complex with a number of extensions, including an accommodation block containing 24 en suite bedrooms. There are two comfortable lounge bars, with specially furnished separate settle seating and pretty wallpaper. The Vivaldi Restaurant is appropriately decorated with musical instruments and an unusually interesting à la carte menu is served here. The standard of service is high and the atmosphere in all parts of the hotel is very friendly. The extensive grounds have a garden section equipped with well-constructed play equipment for the use of children.

This is a freehouse and the bar offers Webster's Yorkshire Bitter, John Smith's Bitter, Ruddles Best Bitter, Marston's Pedigree, Foster's Australian beer, Strongbow cider, Carlsberg lager and Kaliber alcohol-free lager. The bar food includes home-made soup, garlic mushrooms, prawn cocktail or melon and raspberries for starters. Jacket potatoes with various fillings, omelettes, home-cooked ham, egg and chips and the special of the day are also on the menu. Grills on offer include grilled gammon with egg or pineapple, Four Seasons mixed grill and fish dishes such as whole grilled trout, deep fried scampi, cod or haddock. Among the restaurant menu's starters are chicken liver pâté, devilled whitebait, Chinese dim-sum, and mushroom surprise. There are main courses such as poached salmon served with a dill and cucumber sauce, lemon sole thermidor, filled with crab and scallops poached in white wine, chicken Hawaiian, duck Carolina, quail royale, roast guinea fowl and chicken Duberge, plus a marvellous selection of specially made sweets. Food is served from 12 noon until 1.45 pm and from 7 pm until 9 pm.

The hotel is open for drinks on Monday to Saturday from 12 noon to 2.30 pm and from 6.30 pm to 11 pm, and on Sunday from 12 noon to 3 pm and 7 pm to 10.30 pm.

Telephone: 01673 860108.

How to get there: The Four Seasons is situated at the crossroads of the Dunholme bypass on the A46 Lincoln to Grimsby road, 10 miles south-west of Market Rasen or 6 miles north-east of Lincoln.

Parking: There is a very large car park at the Four Seasons and it has been agreed that patrons may leave their cars there while they are doing the walk. Some limited roadside parking is available by the triangle containing the war memorial, opposite the church.

Length of the walk: 1½ miles or 3½ miles. Map: OS Landranger sheet 121 Lincoln and surrounding area (inn GR 026790).

Dunholme, saved nowadays by the bypass, is a quiet backwater of a village with an old church and churchyard, shaded by beech and chestnut, sited near the clear waters of the beck flowing down to join the infant Langworth river. The walk takes you through a nature reserve, the gift of a local inhabitant, and along the ancient Ashing Lane, once a cart route across the ford to a long forgotten railway halt.

The Walk

Turn left out of the Four Seasons exit route to walk forward to the old main road. Cross the road and turn right, with the Lord Nelson pub on your left. Turn left over the footbridge across the beck by the church entrance and left again to follow the tarmac path along the beckside. At the ford turn right for about 80 yards, then left at the T-junction and on to the signposted public footpath. Walk forward to climb the stile and continue, with the fence on your right, to the next stile. Turn right after crossing the stile to walk along the wide track over the field and go right again at the path junction on a signposted bridleway. On meeting the Market Rasen road again, turn left for about 170 yards to Beck Lane.

For the shorter walk: Cross the footbridge at the side of the ford and, at the lane junction, turn right to follow the lane back to the start.

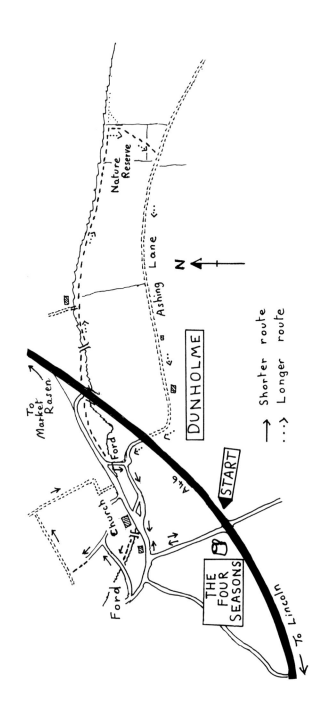

Nature Reserve

Ashing Lane

DUNHOLME

→ Shorter route
⋯⋯⟩ Longer route

N

To Market Rasen

Ford

A 46

START

Church

Ford

THE FOUR SEASONS

To Lincoln

For the longer walk: Do not go down Beck Lane, but continue forward a few yards to the Anglian Water pumping station. Follow the sign-posted footpath, with the hedge on your immediate left and the allotment area on the right. Continue on the mown track to the signpost and footbridge at the right-hand corner of the field. Cross the bypass road to the stile by the 'Dunholme' road sign and go diagonally left for a few yards to the footbridge.

Cross the bridge and turn left, with the beck on your left, for about 1,000 yards until you reach Pickering Meadow nature reserve, with its instruction about the route, 'Welcome to the Meadow. Please keep to mown paths from March until October'. Walk forward and turn right at the next stile, by the seats, to follow the mown path across the meadow to the entrance gap between the hedges and an earth bridge. Cross the next paddock to a wooden fieldgate, with a stile on the right, to turn right along Ashing Lane.

Follow the lane along for about ¾ mile until you reach the main road. Proceed directly across the road and go down the embankment slope with its non-slip bricks, to follow Ashing Lane, signposted as a bridleway. Continue past the new churchyard and the war memorial to rejoin your earlier route and return to the Four Seasons car park.

⑯ Minting
The Sebastopol Inn

The present brick frontage of the Sebastopol Inn merely re-surfaces, in parts, a much earlier mud and stud structure reputed to be 400 years old. In the past it was an old coaching inn on the way to the coast and the stabling survives today. It is said that a magistrate named the inn during an inquest into the death of a man who had been drowned in the beck in 1855. At that time the inn was known quite simply as 'the beerhouse' and the coroner insisted that a proper name was necessary for his records, so they promptly named it after the siege British soldiers were fighting in that year.

At the time of my preparation for the new edition of this book, the Sebastopol was closed and up for sale. It may re-open of course, but in the meantime the walk from it is still an excellent one and, should you find the pub closed when you arrive, there is a good alternative. This is the Midge Inn, which is two and a quarter miles away at the turn off for Minting from the A158 main road. So it is the Midge Inn whose description follows, but the walk begins from outside the Sebastopol in Minting village itself, where you will need to return after your meal – vice versa if you plan to eat after walking.

Handy for the coast road (but a really welcome respite from it), the Midge Inn has a friendly relaxed atmosphere. There is adequate car parking, with entry from the lane leading to Minting, some picnic tables and a grass area.

Abbotts Ale, Brains Bitter, Mansfield Dark Mild, Doddington's Draught Bitter and Bass are served on handpump in this real ale freehouse. Draught Guinness, Merrydown Draught Cider and Carling Black Label lager, offer additional choice. Chilled wine by the glass is also available.

Food is not served on Mondays or Tuesdays, but at other times bar and restaurant meals, including vegetarian dishes, are served at lunch and in the evenings; certainly more interesting in style and character than the astronaut's dehydrated meals, displayed in a case on the wall!

Telephone: 01507 578348.

How to get there: The Sebastopol is situated in the village of Minting, 1½ miles off the main Lincoln to Horncastle A158 (T) road, some 4½ miles east of Wragby and some 6 miles from Horncastle.

Parking: In the village itself, parking is limited, so please observe the usual courtesies and ensure no obstruction is caused.

Length of the walk: 1½ miles. Map: OS Landranger sheet 122 Skegness area (inn GR 187736).

Off the main tourist route to the coast, this is an easy walk through quiet, country lanes and across an ancient Benedictine site.

The Walk

Turn right out of the inn doorway between the buildings to the road and right again at the road for a few yards. Turn right back again over the beck and, almost immediately, turn left behind the house to a stile. There is a pond on your right. Proceed diagonally right, skirting the pond edge, to a stile in the corner of the field (sometimes muddy). Cross three stiles, visible from one another, and then turn left down to the lane. Turn right down the lane, with the converted chapel on your right.

At the T-junction continue forward down Minting Lane, with Manor Farm drive on your right. At the next T-junction turn right down Pinfold Lane. Turn right again, through the wooden fieldgate just beyond the first bungalow on your right. Walk across the rough pasture, keeping the Sebastopol on your left and, at the bend in the

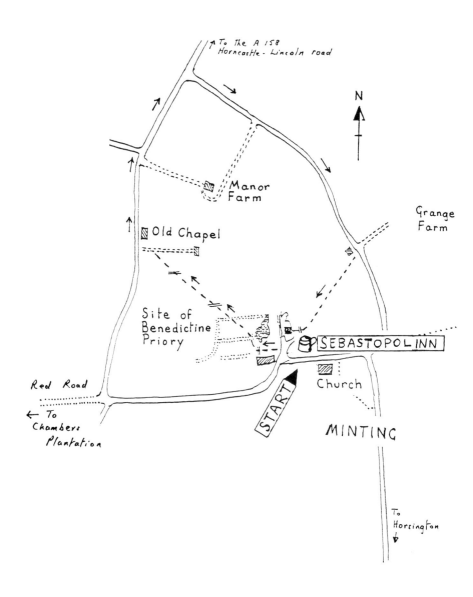

hedge line to your front, you will discover a narrow passage and, hopefully, a stile. This public right of way has the Old School on the right and the garden of a house on the left. Turn left at the green, going over the bridge and back to the car park.

Other places of interest: There is a 'there and back' walk down Red Road, an unsurfaced green lane, to Chambers Plantation and then a choice of colour-coded Forestry Commission walks of varying lengths along waymarked routes. This is an 800 acre forest with oak, ash, silver birch, Scots pine and many other types of conifer. It is 1 ½ miles to the woods, plus the length of any selected route and, of course, 1 ½ miles back to Minting.

Belchford
The Blue Bell

17

The Blue Bell is in the small village of Belchford in the Area of Outstanding Natural Beauty at the very heart of the Lincolnshire Wolds. The inn is over 200 years old, with a lounge bar boasting two open fireplaces, one at each end of the room. There is a marvellous array of interesting woodworking and country craft tools decorating the walls, including an old yoke for carrying pails. The dining area is a snug alcove at one end of the lounge bar. The Viking Way long-distance recreational path actually passes the door and walkers are made most welcome.

Richard and Maureen Geddes have gained the pub a steady reputation for friendly service and good value bar food, that nowadays goes far beyond only catering for the local farming community. Home-made soup, cold ham off the bone, local grilled trout, home-made steak and onion pie or cottage pie and a range of salads, ham, fish or cheese are always available. A selection of sandwiches and a vegetarian dish named Rusty's Pasta are also on the menu. The Blue Bell is a freehouse with beers constantly changing. Examples of what may be on offer are Tetley Keg Bitter, Ansells Mild, Ansells Bitter, Carlsberg Export and Carlsberg lagers, Old English draught cider and Draught

Guinness. Although there is no family room, the very large play paddock is a magnet for children on fine days and there are picnic tables in the garden behind the pub. Dogs are not allowed indoors.

The pub is open on Monday to Saturday from 11 am to 3 pm and 7 pm to 11 pm, and on Sunday from 12 noon to 3 pm and 7 pm to 10.30 pm. Meals are served daily from 12 noon to 2.30 pm and 7.30 pm to 9.30 pm. Booking in advance for Sundays would be appreciated.

Telephone: 01507 533602.

How to get there: Turn off the A153 Horncastle to Louth road 2 miles north of West Ashby or, from the other direction, 3 miles south of Scamblesby. Approaching from the Bluestone Heath Road to the east, turn off down Belchford Hill.

Parking: Customers may park in the Blue Bell inn car park, preferably in the rear car park and furthest away from the entrance. Alternatively, if it is not a Sunday, there is limited parking further along the road at the church entrance at the side of the notice forbidding parking in the village hall car park.

Length of the walk: 4½ miles. Map: OS Landranger sheet 122 Skegness area (inn GR 292755).

Lincolnshire can be seen at its best on this varied circular walk, with the ever-changing colours of the field patterns across the Wold and some magnificent views en route. Over 20 miles away, Lincoln cathedral, set high upon its hill, may be spied from Fulletby Top and the line of the distant river Trent can be followed by a number of power stations' 'mushroom clouds'.

The Walk

From the Blue Bell car park turn left and almost immediately right up Dams Lane, signposted 'The Viking Way'. After following the lane round the bend, turn left over a stile on a signposted path, just before the gate across the track leading to Dams Farm. Walk down to the next stile, cross the footbridge and then turn right. Cross the next stile and turn left, with the fence on your left until the end of the field. Turn right and continue along the hedge line until you meet another signpost and stile.

Walk across to the hedge diagonally left and continue along the field edge, with the hedge on your immediate right. Cross through the hedge and walk up to the top corner of the upper field where there is a stile. Climb the stile and turn left on a good track for a few yards and then right, to proceed downhill with the hedge on your right.

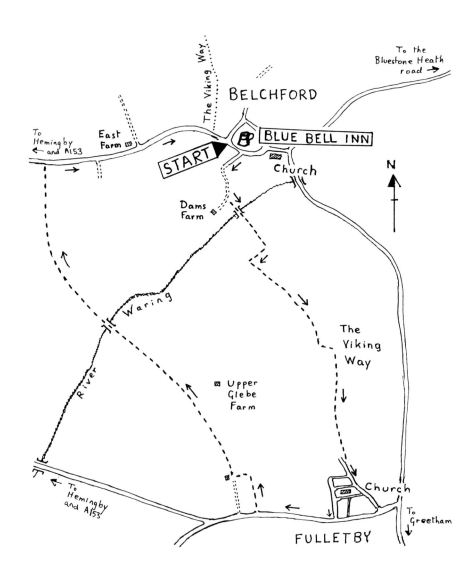

To the
Bluestone Heath
road →

BELCHFORD

The Viking Way

East
Farm

To
Hemingby
and A153

START

BLUE BELL INN

Church

N

Dams
Farm

Waring

River

Upper
Glebe
Farm

The
Viking
Way

Church

To Hemingby
and A153

To
Greetham

FULLETBY

Cross the stiles and bridge and walk up to the top right-hand corner of the field by the bungalow. Turn left, uphill, along the lane and then right, with the church on your right. Turn left at the end of the village lane up to the main road. Turn right past the garage and keep right at the road junction. Turn right down the first track on the right (not as shown on the OS map) and follow this track round to the right past the Old Rectory.

Go through the metal fieldgate and, where the obvious track bends to the right towards the buildings of Upper Glebe Farm, continue forward, with the hedge on your left, to a gate and stile. The route of the bridleway is clearly defined down the next two fields, for it is really a 30 ft wide Inclosure Award path that leads you down to a stout bridge across the infant river Waring. After crossing the bridge, walk straight forward, uphill, on a defined right of way over the arable field that used to be Belchford Common. Continue, with the hedge on the left, along the good track to the road. At the road turn right, and walk down into Belchford village and your starting place.

18 South Thoresby
The Vine Inn

The present Vine Inn building appears to be 18th century with a recent addition, although records of an ale-house go back to 1508. This real ale, freehouse, now run by Kevin and Beverley Cooper, was formerly a blacksmith's shop, general store, post office and always a village institution. It is a friendly and simple place, situated at the edge of a small, comparatively remote village on the very beginnings of the Lincolnshire Wolds and only 7 miles from the sea.

There is a comfortable, old-fashioned lounge, a snug bar, a pool-room and a tiny dining-room (a no smoking area). Outside there is a large old world garden. Overnight accommodation is also available. The bar is well stocked with beer from Lincolnshire's own brewery at Wainfleet – Bateman – plus a variety of guest beers, Carlsberg lager, draught cider and an extensive range of malt whiskies. Bar snacks include soup with roll and butter, freshly cut sandwiches, toasted sandwiches, baps, chip butties, ploughman's (ham, cheese or pâté), beefburger bap or jumbo· sausages in French bread. The dining-room offers, as starters, soup, pâté, whitebait, prawn cocktail, garlic mushrooms and seafood au gratin. Main course meals range from fish dishes to duckling à l'orange, gammon and pineapple, home-made steak and kidney pie, shepherd's pie and lasagne. Salads and vegetarian dishes are available and a variety of desserts.

The inn is open on Monday to Saturday from 12 noon to 11 pm and on Sunday from 12 noon to 3 pm and 7 pm to 10.30 pm. Telephone: 01507 480273.

How to get there: Turn off the A16 (T) Louth to Ulceby Cross road, 1½ miles north-west of Ulceby Cross or, coming from Louth, 3 miles after passing through Burwell. The Vine Inn is the first building on the edge of the village on the only through road.

Parking: The landlord does not mind customers leaving their cars in the inn car park while they do the walk, but do please ask where, for otherwise delivery lorries may have difficulty in negotiating the turn. There is limited alternative parking for one or two cars by the church, if it is not a Sunday.

Length of the walk: 2 miles or 3½ miles. Map: OS Landranger sheet 122 Skegness area (inn GR 401769).

A walk full of interest for nature lovers. The steep sides and wide bottom of the Swaby valley indicate that this was a glacial overflow channel. The valley itself is a Site of Special Scientific Interest for the dry, chalky soil on the valley sides supports old chalk grassland, rare today in Lincolnshire. Controlled grazing encourages plants such as wild thyme and small scabious while the rich marsh in the valley bottom in its undrained state provides good habitat for snipe and lapwing.

The Walk

Turn left out of the inn car park towards the church and right at the lane junction. There are two signposted paths beyond the church – take the right-hand one. Bear left across the paddock to the stile in the fence by the ancient sycamore and then walk towards the old wind pump, keeping it just on your right, with the stream and lakes below on your left. Cross the stile in the left-hand corner of the field by Belleau Bridge, then turn left uphill.

For the shorter walk: Continue for 350 yards. At the right-hand bend in the road turn left on to the good, signposted bridleway track towards a woodland belt. After about 700 yards along this green lane, at the path junction (waymark), turn left and leave the bridleway. Continue from the final paragraph.

For the longer walk: Continue until the end of the wood on the right and then turn right into the field on the signposted footpath, to follow the field edge, with the wood on your right, for 150 yards (the path

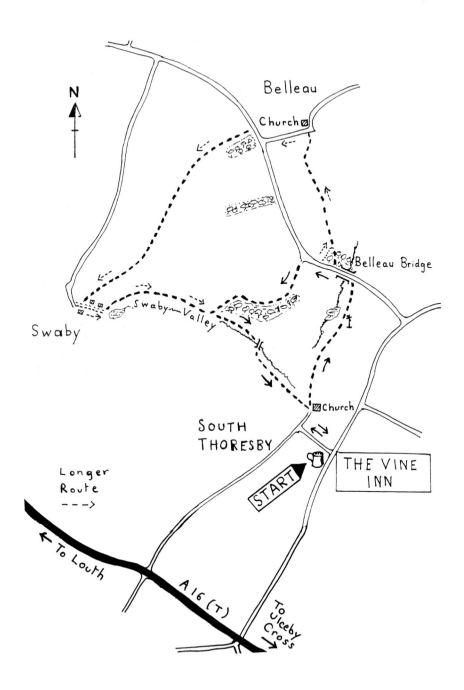

Belleau

Church

Belleau Bridge

Swaby

Swaby Valley

SOUTH
THORESBY

Church

THE VINE
INN

START

Longer
Route
- - - >

To Louth

A16 (T)

To
Ulceby
Cross

N

really should go through the wood but the farmer has kindly marked out this route on his land). At the signpost by the wood edge, turn left across the arable field, aiming towards Belleau church, with the fence on your right. A stile has been made in the field corner. Cross the steep little valley and continue forward towards the church, with the fence on your right. By the church there is a signpost, stile and some steps that have recently been constructed by the farmer. On reaching the lane, turn left to the T-junction.

Turn right again and by the wood turn left off the road, with the wood on your left, to cross the arable field, making at first for the small triangular copse. Aim for the right-hand side of the copse and then walk forward towards the field boundary hedge, just to the right of the corner. Carry on across a large field, keeping the woodland belt over on your left. In the left-hand corner of this field cross the hedge and fence and go down the steep little path at the edge of the wood to the new stile on the lane. Turn left up the lane past the houses into the Swaby valley on a good track. Continue until you meet the shorter route (waymark) joining from the left.

Follow the public footpath, with the stream below the bank on your right. Walk along the field edge until you come to the footbridge on your right, cross the bridge and go over the duckboards on the far bank. Turn left at the top of the bank to walk towards South Thoresby church across this deliberately undrained marshy section. Go over the stepping blocks and on to the stile. Continue forward towards the church and go over the stile into the lane, retracing your steps to the car park.

Tealby
The King's Head

The 14th century King's Head makes a very pretty picture with its rare thatched roof and charming surroundings in a village considered by many to be the most beautiful in the Wolds. The pub is one of the oldest inns in the county, ably managed today by Ray and Lyn Miller. Ray is a trained chef and his last major appointment before becoming a licensee was on the Cunard luxury liner Queen Elizabeth II. The two-page menu should satisfy all-comers with delicious, reasonably priced meals, ranging from home-made steak and kidney and chicken and ham pies to Tealby sausages, smoked mackerel, or breast of chicken with an onion, mushroom and wine sauce served with rice. Vegetarian dishes are available as are salads and a range of sandwiches. The pub is a freehouse serving Ruddles, Directors and John Smith's beer and Scrumpy Jack cider. There is a no-smoking area, a large beer garden with a dozen tables widely scattered around, a family room and a garden for young children. Well-behaved dogs are welcome.

From Monday through to Saturday it is open from 11.30 am to 3 pm and from 6 pm to 11 pm. On Sundays it opens from 12 noon to 3 pm and from 7 pm to 10.30 pm.

Telephone: 01673 838347.

How to get there: Tealby lies 4 miles from Market Rasen on the B1203 Grimsby road. If approaching on the B1225 (known as Caistor High Street) turn off at Bully Hill crossroads, some 7 miles from Caistor, steeply downhill into Tealby.

Parking: Parking is available in the large car park at the King's Head for customers doing the walk, but it is only courteous to mention it to the landlord. An alternative parking place is the large car park at the Tennyson D'Enycourt Memorial Hall (the village hall).

Length of the walk: 3½ miles. Map: OS Landranger sheet 113 Grimsby and surrounding area (inn GR 157905).

The fine Norman church of All Saints with its interesting memorials and Tennyson connections stands grandly above the peaceful village through which the infant river Rase flows down from Bully Hill. Indeed, the colourful lane leading down to the ford by the village hall must be as picturesque as any village street in England. There are exhilarating views, with Lincoln cathedral in the distance, and some quite steep sections that belie the widely-held belief that Lincolnshire is flat. The walk is in an Area of Outstanding Natural Beauty (AONB) on the very edge of the Wolds, partly along one of the best sections of the Viking Way long distance recreational path and through a Countryside Commission Stewardship Site with unlimited public access.

The Walk

Turn left out of the car park and keep to the right round the bend in the lane. A few yards past the butcher's, turn right down the alleyway labelled 'The Smootings' that quickly becomes a very attractive stream-side path.

Turn left uphill at the lane past the Memorial Hall on the right and cross the main road. Climb the steps on the left by the Caistor Lane roadsign into the churchyard and follow the path round to the steps behind the church.

Turn right at the lane for 40 yards and then go left, uphill, on the good signposted track. Take the blue metal fieldgate (waymarked) to the left of the house and then go diagonally right across the paddock to the concealed stile in the dip at the far right-hand corner of the field. A wonderful panorama may be seen across Willingham Forest over on the left. Climb the stile and continue forward, with the hedge on your right, and then across the field towards North Wold Farm, with an odd bend in the path as you near the farm. Go through the wooden fieldgate into the farmyard and turn right up the farm track to the road.

At the road turn left for 350 yards along Caistor Lane and then go

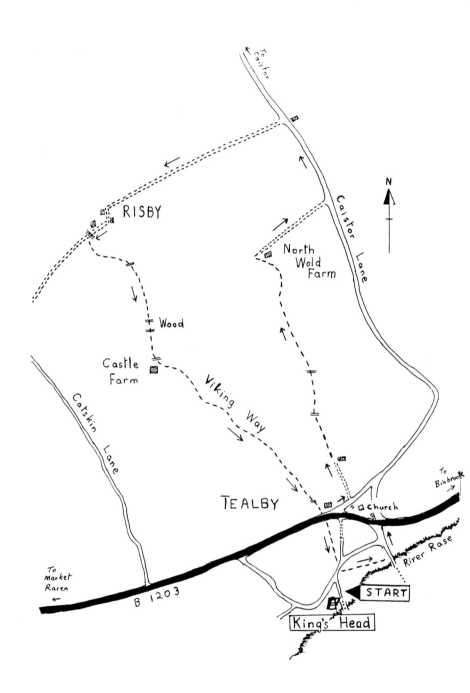

left up the signposted bridleway opposite the farm buildings. The bridleway is clearly marked through Risby Farm buildings and, upon reaching the cattle grid just beyond the farmhouse, turn left along the Landrover track that is the Viking Way. The fields here are in a ten year conservation plan under the Countryside Commission Stewardship Scheme.

At the metal fieldgate and stile proceed diagonally left, uphill, to a stile in the corner of the field by the wood. Walk along the clear path by the wood edge and, at the end of the wood by Castle Farm, cross the stile and proceed left along the right-hand slope of the steep valley to the metal fieldgate and waymark in the extreme right-hand corner of the field. Continue to follow the field edge, with the hedge on your right and some enormous boulders. Cross the stile in the field corner to the right of the house. Go over the main road and take the signposted footpath directly opposite to follow the field edge, with a hedge now on your immediate left. At the stile and signpost by the lane, turn right to the King's Head car park.

Other places of interest: A mile south-west down the road at Tealby Thorpe there is a working watermill.

The Ramblers' church at Walesby, north-west of Tealby, on a medieval village site, is worth a visit and is always open.

Donington on Bain
The Black Horse

20

The 18th century Black Horse is a real ale pub under the enthusiastic management of Tony and Janine Pacey and transformed in recent years. It is situated in the pleasant village of Donington on Bain in the valley of the river Bain, with the landmarks of the Belmont TV mast on one side and the obsolescent Stenigot radar saucers on the other. The Viking Way long distance recreational path actually passes the pub door.

The lounge bar has old beams, an open fire in winter and three attractive inglenooks, plus a large, separate dining area. There is also a games room with a pool table. Dogs should remain outside, but they will be quite happy with their surroundings – there are lots of picnic tables in a good-sized, sheltered beer garden and an area with swings where children may safely play. Tony asks that you leave muddy footwear outside too. En-suite accommodation is also available here in a modern block containing eight twin rooms.

The drinks on offer are well-kept Courage Directors, Webster's Green Label Best and Foster's draught. There is also Draught Guinness, Dry Blackthorn cider and Miller Pilsner lager. Bar snacks include sandwiches, jacket potatoes with various fillings, prawns and cheese and ploughman's. Main course meals range from Viking Grill – gammon, sausage, egg, pineapple, mushrooms and onion rings – to trout in a white sauce, various pizzas and steak dishes. Vegetarian food is also provided. There is a separate menu for children. The special dish of the day is shown on a blackboard and there is always a full range of sweets, one of which is named Black Horse Treat.

The pub is open on Monday to Saturday from 11 am to 3 pm and 7 pm to 11 pm, and on Sunday from 12.30 pm to 3 pm and 7 pm to 10.30 pm. Last orders for lunches are taken at 2 pm, and for evening meals at 10 pm on weekdays and 9.30 pm on Sundays.

Telephone: 01507 343640.

How to get there: Donington on Bain is signposted eastwards off the Caistor to Horncastle road (High Street), the B1225, surely one of the most scenically attractive roads in the county, some 11 miles from Horncastle or 14 miles from Caistor. The village is 1½ miles down the hill, south-east of the Belmont TV mast that dominates the countryside for miles around.

Parking: Customers may park in the very large car park. Some roadside parking (with care) may be possible in the village, off the main through road.

Length of the walk: Total length 3½ miles. It is a figure-of-eight walk, with Walk A being 1¼ miles and Walk B 2¼ miles. Map: OS Landranger sheet 122 Skegness area (inn GR 237829).

The high wolds encompass this village, with its much photographed watermill, in the valley of the little river Bain. The walk is partly along the valley towards Benniworth Haven and the squat, unbuttressed tower of the 700-year-old Doningtonn church may be seen for much of the walk. The brief climb between Horseshoe and Horsebottom Plantations is amply rewarded by the extensive views from the top of the Wolds.

The Walk

Walk A: Turn right out of the car park, with the village hall and the church on your right, to walk towards the Belmont TV mast, which stands 1,265 ft high. Turn left up Old School Lane opposite the church, with Neve Gardens on the right. Continue to the end of this little lane to a signpost and step stile for a path leading down to the beck. Cross the stile and ditchboard to follow the path round to the left to another stile and then a proper footbridge and a white handgate.

Walk up towards Benniworth House Farm, bearing slightly left to

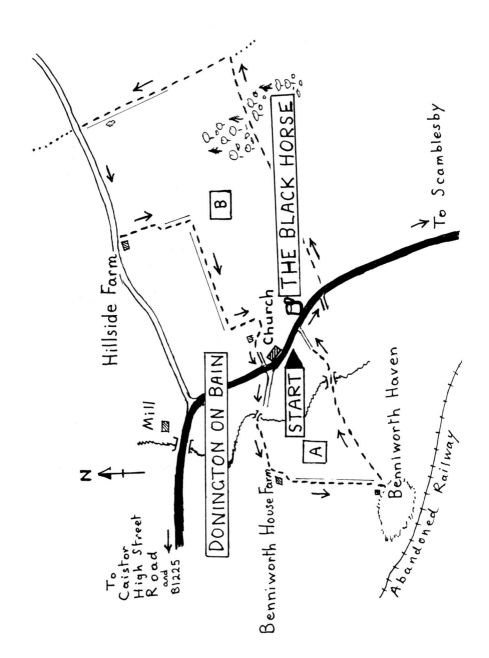

N

To
Caistor
High Street
Road
and
B1225

Mill

Hillside Farm

DONINGTON ON BAIN

B

Church

THE BLACK HORSE

To Scamblesby

START

A

Benniworth House Farm

Benniworth Haven

Abandoned Railway

86

the tall triple signpost for the diverted bridleway (not as shown on the OS map) and then diagonally left to the fieldgate and stile. Turn left here, with the hedge on your immediate right.

At the end of the field our way is to the left down into the valley but it is worth going on for 50 yards to look at the large pond known as Benniworth Haven and then returning to this stile. Climb the stile and walk downhill to a bridge over the river and look at the English Heritage plaque, 'Well preserved riverside meadow with no artificial inputs in order to enhance the natural flora and fauna.'

Walk along the proper track by the sewage plant, cross the farm track and continue forward, with the hedge on your left, to a step stile and waymark. Turn left when you meet a line of cupressus across your front and left again at the path junction. Turn right down the track to the road, ignoring the signpost and stile on your left, to continue down Chapel Lane to the main street of the village.

Walk B: Turn left out of the Black Horse car park and walk along the main road for about 350 yards. Opposite Meadowcroft turn left over the stile on a signposted footpath. It is often a bit muddy, due to a spring-line, for the first 100 yards by the next stile. Continue uphill, with the hedge on your right, in between the two plantations. As you clear the trees the Stenigot radar saucers come into view over on the right.

Turn left at the track junction and continue until you meet the lane. Turn left downhill along the lane until you reach the edge of Hillside Farm. Turn left along the diverted path with the fence on your right, until you reach the stile. Climb the stile and turn left along the field edge with the hedge on the left.

Turn right downhill after the small footbridge and almost at the bottom of the field turn sharp left on a clear, waymarked, diverted path. Turn right up a narrow passage, at first between hedges, and by the stables on the right turn right up the flagstone path for 5 yards and then right again into Church Close. Turn left by the church and walk back to the Black Horse.

21 Louth
The Wheatsheaf

The Wheatsheaf was built as a coaching inn in 1625 and retains much of its original character. This charming hostelry nestles almost at the foot of the beautiful St James' church with its superbly proportioned tower and spire, which reaches 295 ft and is claimed to be the highest parish church spire in the land. After a bet made over a flagon of ale a man named Anthony Fountain climbed to the top of the spire in 1771 and another, Benjamin Smith, after drinking ten pints of ale, succeeded in tying a handkerchief round the iron which supports the weathercock in 1818. The original weathercock on the spire was fixed in 1515 amid great rejoicing for it was made from a copper basin which was part of the booty captured at Flodden Field from James IV of Scotland. John Betjeman wrote, 'This magnificent church is one of the last great medieval masterpieces.'

There are three low-beamed, snug rooms with an open fireplace in the lounge bar, photographs of old Louth on the walls, interesting clocks and a malt shovel on display. In the yard behind the inn there are picnic tables and a red telephone box. The real ale includes Boddingtons Bitter, Flowers Original and Bentley's Yorkshire Bitter, and the lagers are Heineken, Stella Artois and Carling Black Label.

There is Draught Guinness and Murphy's Stout, as well as a good choice of wine. Among the freshly made and varied bar meals are the Wheatsheaf ploughman's lunch, French bread, ham and salad, a range of sandwiches, home-made moussaka served with rice and chopped salad, lasagne verdi, home-made chicken curry and steak and kidney pie.

The inn is open on Monday through to Saturday from 11 am to 11 pm, and on Sunday from 12 noon to 3 pm and 7 pm to 10.30 pm. No food is available on Sundays and a limited menu on Saturdays. However, full bar meals are served on Mondays to Fridays from 12 noon to 2 pm.

Telephone: 01507 606262.

How to get there: A route centre, Louth is 27 miles from Lincoln on the A157, 14 miles from Horncastle on the A153 and 15 miles from Market Rasen on the A631. It is also some 14 miles from the coast. The new bypass for coast traffic means that the town centre is less disturbed nowadays than it was in the past. The Wheatsheaf is in Westgate at the foot of the church tower.

Parking: Customers may park in the inn car park but space is limited. No convenient roadside parking is in the immediate vicinity but there are a number of municipal car parks in town with varying charges. However, as it is a circular walk it would be possible to leave a car in Hubbard's Hills car park (marked on the sketch map by Dog Kennel Farm – turn up Love Lane and right at the top to continue to the end of a cul-de-sac) and walk to the Wheatsheaf en route.

Length of the walk: 3 miles. Map: OS Landranger sheet 113 Grimsby and surrounding area (inn GR 326874).

A delightfully contrasting town and country walk in this 'jewel of a town', beloved by John Betjeman. The lovely beech trees in the wooded gorge of Hubbard's Hills, the superb, crocketed spire of St James' church and the river Lud, flowing through this enchanted valley on its meandering way to the sea at Grainthorpe Haven, may all be seen and enjoyed during this walk.

The Walk
Turn left out of the car park and follow Westgate round to the left and then along the footway over the green on your left. Cross the bridge and turn left immediately, up to the attractive old graveyard where the gravestones are stacked five deep along the wall. Walk diagonally right across the open space to turn left at the road and go on to the Louth town sign. Turn left again towards Westgate, cross the bridge and the

89

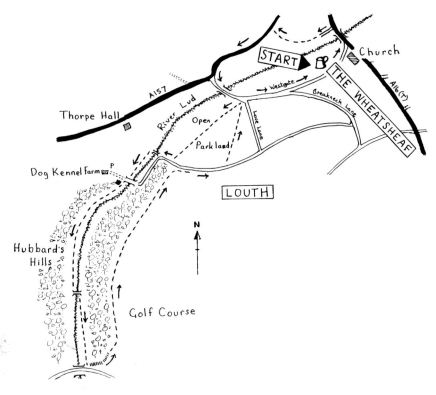

road to the white painted fence and handgate at the beginning of Love Lane.

Walk along the tarmac path across the beautiful open parkland and turn right when you meet the lane. Continue along this lane for 100 yards and, just beyond the bend, cross over the river and walk forward, with the river Lud now on your left. Turn right on meeting .the lane again and almost immediately left down the concrete slope by the toilets at the entrance to Hubbard's Hills. Car parking and a restaurant are available here.

Walk forward through the valley, with the precipitous slope on your left, and continue on the good path, with the river at first on your left and then on your right. At the end of the park turn left up the steep flight of steps and, five steps from the top, turn left again up some more steps to follow the high level path at the top of 'the cliff', with the beech trees clothing the steep slope on your left and a golf course on the right.

On coming down to the lane, continue forward, past the gate where you joined the route earlier and round the bend for 400 yards to a stile on the left. Climb the stile and walk across the parkland to the white painted handgate on Love Lane. Turn right along the main road as far as the junction with Breakneck Lane and then go left up Westgate back to the Wheatsheaf. Spare some time to explore historic Louth, if you can.

Other places of interest: At the side of the road on the bridge near the church are the remains of an old mill with its mill race and a plaque indicating the height of the flood level in May, 1920 when the river rose 15 ft after a cloud burst and many people were drowned.

The Greenwich Meridian passes through Louth and it is marked by a plaque on a shop in Eastgate and a metal strip on the pavement.

By the church is a plaque commemorating the vicar, Thomas Kendall, who was hanged at Tyburn for taking part in the Lincolnshire Rising in 1536.

22 Little Cawthorpe
The Royal Oak

Little Cawthorpe is an attractive village whose small population, tucked away on the edge of the Wolds, is almost the same as it was 150 years ago. Only one farm remains today out of the five that were operating 50 years ago. The village has, in the past, won the Lincolnshire Best Kept Small Village Competition and an oak tree, planted on the grassy area near the Royal Oak, was the prize donated to the village.

The Royal Oak, nicknamed 'The Splash' because of the ford, is run with enthusiasm by Robin Scarfe, assisted by the resident manager, Sue Connor. Major renovations and improvements to the pub are in hand but at present, this old, low-beamed pub is full of delightful nooks and crannies. It has an enormous brick fireplace in one of the alcoves off the lounge bar and, in season, actually two open fires. There are vintage photographs and hunting prints on the walls. There is an arcaded, tiled out-of-doors bar area, picnic tables in the garden and a children's play area with equipment. 'The Splash' enjoys a good reputation for its high standard of service and its food, among both locals and visitors from miles around. Well-kept Ind Coope Burton Ale, Courage Directors and Ruddles County are served with Carlsberg Export and Castlemaine XXXX draught lager and Scrumpy Jack cider. Good helpings of freshly made bar food include sandwiches, soup and ploughman's, and, more substantially, stir-fry, turkey cordon bleu, Scotch salmon steak or vegetarian dishes are all available. On Sundays there are traditional lunches.

The pub is open at lunchtime from 12 noon to 3 pm and in the evening from 7 pm to 11 pm (10.30 pm on Sunday). Meals are normally served from 12 noon until 2 pm and from 7 pm until 9.30 pm.

Telephone: 01507 600750.

How to get there: Little Cawthorpe is signposted off the A157 Louth to Mablethorpe road, 3 miles south-east of Louth.

Parking: The Royal Oak has a large car park and the licensee does not mind customers leaving their cars while they are doing the walk.

Length of the walk: 1½ miles. Map: OS Landranger sheet 122 Skegness area (inn GR 359840).

Lying in a hollow with woods all around, Little Cawthorpe is an enchanting village with twisting lanes around central fields, a pleasant stream, an abandoned railway and a charming old manor house. It is an ancient place, for the priory was founded in the 12th century, although there are only earth mounds remaining today. The source of the Long Eau is here, from seven springs that have now been made into an attractive pond favoured by mallards and moorhens. Locals still call the area by the church 'The Springs'. A resident on Water Lane, by the Royal Oak, has logged 80 species of birds over the years, including nightingales, the lesser spotted woodpecker and tawny owls.

The Walk

Turn right out of the car park down to the ford with its footbridge on the left. Turn right down Water Lane, with the Long Eau on your right. Cross the left footbridge at the end of the lane and proceed straight forward up Wood Lane for some 350 yards.

Turn right off Wood Lane on the signposted path at the end of the hedge on your right, to a metal fieldgate and a stile. Walk on to a step stile in the left-hand corner of the paddock. Cross the next field also to the left-hand corner and turn right for 10 yards to a footbridge and stile. Turn left after crossing the bridge, almost into the field corner, with the hedge on your left. After negotiating the stile walk straight across the arable field and then diagonally right to a footbridge and

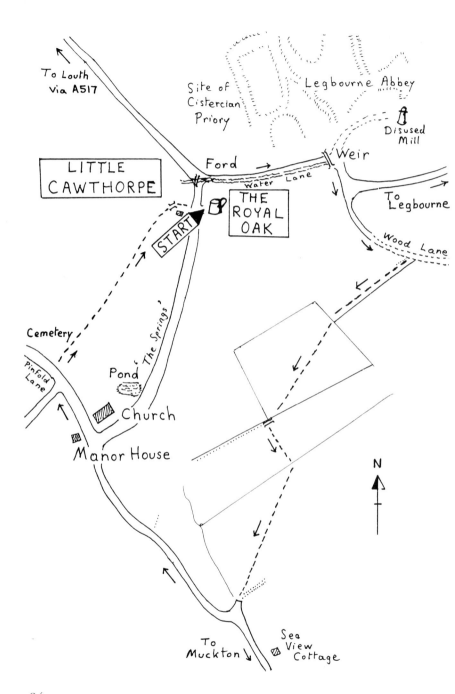

To Louth
via A517

Site of
Cistercian
Priory

Legbourne Abbey

Disused
Mill

Ford →

Weir

LITTLE
CAWTHORPE

Water Lane

THE
ROYAL
OAK

To
Legbourne

START

Wood Lane

Cemetery

'The Springs'

Pond

Pinfold
Lane

Church

N

Manor House

To
Muckton ↓

Sea
View
Cottage

94

stile. Walk forward towards the trees to a stile and footbridge in the corner and then on to the road. Note the name of the house over on your left, for there are quite spectacular views from this road across the middle marsh to the sea.

Turn right along the road leading back into the village, with the lovely, mellow brick Manor House, whose coat of arms indicates 1673, on your left. 'The Springs' are on the right, just below the little red-brick church, which was built in the late 14th century, restored in the 19th century. Continue walking forward up Pinfold Lane for only a few yards to turn right off the lane, through the white kissing-gate on to a mown path with lots of tree-planting on either side. The path leads you to an odd little concrete bridge at the side of a house. Turn right at the side of the garden and then left up the track, which brings you directly opposite the Royal Oak car park entrance.

23 Theddlethorpe All Saints
The King's Head

What a find! A fascinating pub situated on a back road with only a few houses and farms strung along it and not even in the village. This 15th century thatched inn is worthy of a visit in itself, as well as providing good food and drink. It has an extensive garden, a patio with outdoor tables placed round a genuine well and an old farm cart stationed at the entrance. Although it says 'Mind your head at the low doorway', the ceiling in the lounge bar can only be 5 ft 9 inches high, and even less than that where there are beams. There is a snug bar room with farming and horse equipment displayed on the walls and an attractive lounge bar decorated with copper and brass, with a dining area at one end and a smaller connecting dining-room.

Cyril and Julie Robinson, with in-laws Bill and June Pearce, manage this freehouse, real ale pub and have earned an enviable reputation for good quality, home-cooked meals. A sample of the seafood on the menu is breaded torpedo fantail prawns, plaice goujons, king prawns marinated in garlic and seafood platter. Steak diane with mustard, cream and brandy sauce and steak au poivre are just two of the meat dishes. There is also a full list of bar snacks. We had the prawn sandwiches recommended to us by a couple who said they had been visiting the King's Head for meals for the last 20 years. On offer is a range of well-kept beers, including Bass Mild, Stones Best Bitter, Worthington Best Bitter, Bass Cask Ale, Tennent's Extra, Draught Guinness, Carlsberg Black Label and Blackthorn Dry cider. Chilled wine is also available.

The opening hours are 12 noon until 2 pm and 7 pm until 10 pm throughout the whole week.

Telephone: 01507 338655.

How to get there: From the A1031 Mablethorpe to Cleethorpes coast road turn off at Theddlethorpe St Helen and then go left at Theddlethorpe All Saints crossroads for ½ mile to the King's Head. Approaching from Louth on the B1200 Saltfleetby road, turn right at Saltfleetby St Peter and across the Great Eau river to Theddlethorpe All Saints.

Parking: Customers may park in the large car park of the King's Head while they are doing the walk. There is also some possibility of parking, with care, anywhere along the roadside leading to the King's Head.

Length of the walk: 3 ¾ miles. Map: OS Landranger sheet 113 Grimsby and surrounding area (inn GR 472872).

Theddlethorpe is made up of two parishes, All Saints and St Helen. About ½ mile to the east of St Helen lie the sea and the dunes which form part of Saltfleet Nature Reserve. This was always a smugglers' coast, and farm wagons would carry the untaxed goods, gin and tobacco inland to conceal them on the farms.

This gentle walk leads you along lanes and across fields, with plenty to see along the way. The lovely, redundant church of All Saints, seen across a field during the walk, was handsome enough to have earned a name in the past of 'The Cathedral of the Marsh'.

The Walk

Turn left along the road after leaving the King's Head car park and walk down the road for 450 yards to the curiously named Hand Puddle Hole Bridge. Turn left down the signposted bridleway with Silver Street and a deep dyke on the left. At a track junction turn right (waymark) to the road. Left down Rotten Row passing The Wong telephone box on the left.

At the lane junction turn left onto the main road for about 100 yards then left on a signposted path across the stile and concrete bridge with handrail over the wide Girdidike Drain. Go diagonally right across the field from the stile to another stile, concrete bridge and signpost. Turn

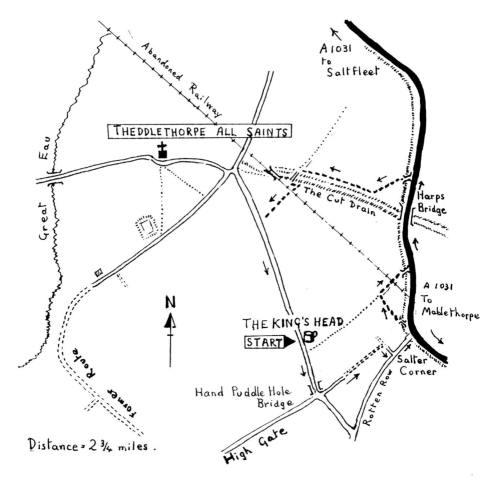

Distance = 2¾ miles.

right along the field edge with a small ditch on your immediate right until you reach a splendid new bridge at the roadside. At the road turn left after crossing to walk along the verge facing the traffic.

After the road bridge turn left off the road over another new wooden bridge and stile and proceed diagonally left across the pasture field to drain edge. On reaching the fence above the Cut Drain turn right along the edge of the field with the drain on your left towards the ruined house on the opposite bank.

On reaching the fieldgate climb the stile and turn left over the new wooden bridge to gain the other bank by the ruined house. Turn left for 6 yards and then right along the field edge to a small footbridge leading onto the lane. Turn left at the lane back to the King's Head.

Other places of interest: Saltfleet Nature Reserve, on the dunes that lie ½ mile to the east of Theddlethorpe St Helen. With its varied habitat the reserve is the home for a wide variety of insects, butterflies, birds and animals, including the rare natterjack toad. The writer D.H. Lawrence was a frequent visitor to the area for the serene sandhills along the foreshore fascinated him.

24 Saltfleet
The New Inn

Saltfleet is an interesting little village that was once the principal port of the Roman province Flavia Caesarienses and the terminus of the great Fosse Way leading all the way to Exeter. The New Inn (which isn't new!) is a fascinating old building that was once a coaching house dating back to the early 1800s. An extension has a date of 1878 scratched upon a window pane.

Being on the coast it comes as no surprise to learn of the long association of the New Inn with the sea. It used to be called the Dolphin and the inn gave shelter to many sailors and merchants using the nearby little port of Saltfleet Haven. 'Traders of the night' were also constant callers, so that:

> *Running round the woodlump, if you chance to find*
> *Little barrels, roped and tarred, all full of brandy wine*
> *Don't shout to come and look, nor take 'em for your play;*
> *Put the brushwood back again – they'll be gone next day.*

In the days of sailing ships there were numerous wrecks along this coast and old stories are still retold locally about ships being

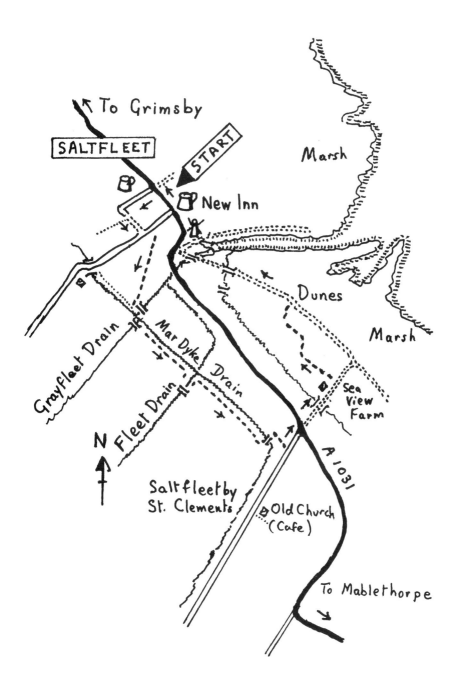

To Grimsby

SALTFLEET

START

New Inn

Marsh

Dunes

Marsh

Grayfleet Drain

Mar Dyke Drain

Fleet Drain

Sea View Farm

N

A 1031

Saltfleetby St. Clements

Old Church (Cafe)

To Mablethorpe

deliberately wrecked off Saltfleet for salvage. All along the coast there were 'salvage sales', much of the timber being used in local building. One such sale was advertised to take place in the New Inn yard in May 1870, with salvage from the wreck of the *Hand of Providence*.

The pub did have twelve letting bedrooms where the gentry used to come for a stay by the seaside. David and Linda Campion do not provide accommodation today but there is an extensive caravan park with a children's play area immediately behind the inn.

The New Inn is a freehouse serving a wide variety of real ales: Bateman; Tom Woods Bomber County; Bass Fine Ale; Bass Mild; Mansfield Bitter; Worthington Draught Bitter; and Stones Bitter. Carling Black Label lager, draught Guinness and Scrumpy Jack cider, plus chilled wine, complete the range of drinks on offer. Good, plain food is served piping hot and may include home-made steak pie, Cumberland sausage, chicken and fish dishes, salads and ploughman's. Vegetarians are also catered for. There is one enormous lounge with a more intimate alcove by a front window, a no smoking area and a beer garden with picnic tables on a grassed area at the front of the inn. Meals are served from 12 noon to 2 pm on Monday to Friday and from 12 noon until 3 pm on Saturday and Sunday. Evening meals are served from 7 pm to 9 pm on Friday and Saturday only.

Telephone: 01507 338068.

How to get there: Saltfleet lies on the main A1031 between Grimsby and Mablethorpe. The New Inn is situated on the main road within yards of the prominent windmill.

Parking: There is ample parking by the New Inn but please park with care as it is a very busy entrance to the caravan park.

Length of the walk: 2¾ miles. Map: OS Landranger sheet 113 Grimsby and surrounding area (inn GR 444938).

A walk of great contrasts across farmland, along wide dykes, over sandhills and through a nature reserve, with glimpses of the sea beyond the samphire marshes.

The Walk

Turn right out of the New Inn along the main road down to the crossroads in 50 yards marked 'The Hill'. Look first though at the signposted Chapel and Garden almost directly opposite the inn. This delightful, well-kept garden is dedicated to the people of the village who lost their lives in the floods of January 1953. Have a look at the inscription on the village pump to Trooper Freshney of the Imperial Light Horse and then turn left down Pump Lane with the Crown Inn on your right. Follow this lane round to the left, with North Creek on your immediate right. Cross the road and the bridge over North Creek to take the signposted diagonal path on the left that has been cleared across the arable field.

Turn left over the old stone bridge, cross the track and then go over the new wooden bridge on the signposted path along the field edge, with the Mar Dyke Drain on your left. At the dyke junction with the Fleet Drain, detour down to the concrete bridge for about 150 yards, cross the drain and return back on the other bank to continue to follow your orginal line. A 52 ft bridge is planned for this crossing.

Towards the end of the field near the lane and Saltfleetby St Clements old church, turn left over the splendid new bridge and follow the path for a few yards over the stile to the road. Turn left at the lane and go straight across the main road to Sea View Farm. Turn left up the wooden steps on the steep bank to follow the signposted path over the stile and then to turn right through the wooden fieldgate into the nature reserve, walking towards the shore at first and then left along the top of the sandhills, with the perimeter fence on your right. The protected ponds on your left are the breeding place of the rare natterjack toad.

In the far right corner of the reserve there are two stiles. Take the right-hand one and scramble down the short bank onto the good public track along the marsh edge. Turn left, walking towards the prominent landmark of the restored mill building. Walk straight across the old stone bridge above the Great Eau outfall and continue to the main road. Note here the signpost for 'Paradise'.

Walk back along the main road past the windmill to the New Inn.

25 Susworth
The Jenny Wren

Not many hamlets are named after a particular person but Susworth is called after a man who, long ago, had a salmon fish farm or 'worth' here. Through the centuries his name has altered from Swyrkeswhod and Swerkeswat to Surrwat, Surswath and finally to Susworth. The Jenny Wren is a real find in this remote area by the side of the river Trent. There was once a wharf here and coal was unloaded for distribution around the district. The pub itself is about 150 years old and the Jenny Wren must surely be one of the friendliest pubs in Lincolnshire. People come to drive through the nearby woods and enjoy the quiet countryside but, more particularly, to experience the hospitality and welcome of the Jenny Wren, where Mark and Alyson Rumbelow are mine hosts.

It has always been important to the Rumbelows to see that their customers get value for money and this is apparent in the quality of the beer and the food. The exceptional bar menu ranges from fresh home-made soup to butterfly shrimps, farmhouse pâté and hot smoked mackerel and prawns sitting in a nest of cottage cheese with slices of avocado. Sandwiches are sliced to order, from either crusty wholemeal or farmhouse white loaves, with a choice of fillings. Hot sandwiches include avocado melt – a triple decker toasted sandwich with avocado and cheese, served with fries. Healthy Harry salad and warm barbecued chicken and bacon salads are also available. These are only the 'While-U-Wait' items, and the main course list is equally interesting. Tagliatelle verdi with fresh spinach and broccoli in a spicy tomato sauce, finished with fresh Parmesan is but one of the vegetarian dishes. Honey roast ham steak accompanied by a poached egg, steak, Guinness and mushroom pie with a puff pastry lid, and a full range of steaks are also available. Omelettes are served at lunchtimes, with the choice of ham and asparagus or farmhouse Cheddar and chives. The range of sweets is just as varied and exciting.

The pub has managed to preserve a cosy and old-fashioned feel and has a number of alcoves around the large lounge bar. It is a freehouse, serving well-kept Smith's, Webster's and Tetley plus one guest beer. Carlsberg Pilsner, Carlsberg Export and Draught Guinness are also on offer. The river bank across the road is used as a beer garden and children are welcome here. There is also a family room and a function room upstairs. Dogs are not permitted indoors.

The pub is open at lunchtimes from 12 noon to 3 pm and in the evenings from 6.30 pm to 11 pm (7 pm to 10.30 pm on Sundays). Bar meals are available from 12 noon to 2 pm and 7 pm to 10 pm.

Telephone: 01724 783441.

How to get there: Turn westwards off the A159 Gainsborough to Scunthorpe road in Scotter village and drive 3 miles down the lane to Susworth.

Parking: The proprietors have readily agreed that customers may leave their cars in the large car park at the Jenny Wren while they are doing the walk. Alternatively, roadside parking may be available, with care, on the lane running parallel to the river.

Length of the walk: 4½ miles. Map: OS Landranger sheet 112 Scunthorpe (inn GR 835021).

An unknown area of the county for many people, this is a walk for nature lovers. The delvings or borrow pits created during the process of bank building along the river Eau have become wildlife habitats containing a variety of plants such as water violets, sweetgrass, flowering rush and water speedwell. They are also home for dragonflies, darterflies and damselflies which may be seen in great abundance. The reeds provide cover for nesting birds such as mallard, swans, coot, tufted duck and moorhens and they may all be seen during the walk.

'Ea' means a stream. About 200 years ago a prehistoric boat was found in these river pastures. In ancient times the river Eau divided into three delta streams,

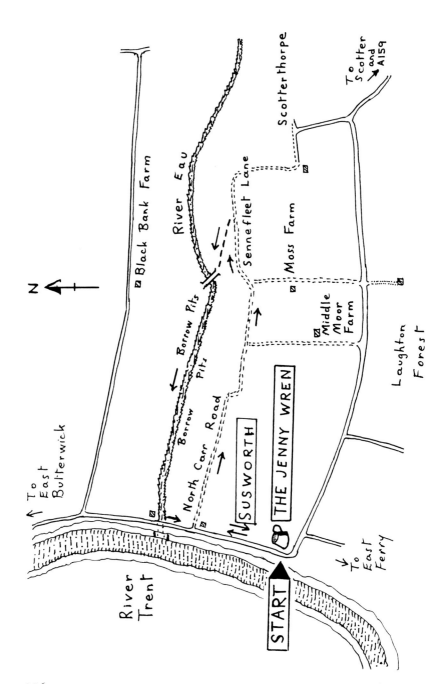

Bellingfleet, Manfleet and the southern one Sennefleet, which originally meant 'the tidal inlet of the island at the junction of the tributary waters'. Sennafleet Lane is very old and this is indicated by the widely different variety of trees in the hedgerow, including apples.

The Walk

Turn right out of the Jenny Wren car park for about a 1,000 yards and then right up the track known as North Carr Road. Do not turn too early onto a farm track.

Follow this track, which becomes Sennefleet Lane round the bend to the left where, after a couple of hundred yards, you will find a stile and signpost on the left. Take this path to the splendid new footbridge, christened by the children of the local primary school at the opening ceremony as 'Beggars Hill Bridge'.

Cross the bridge and turn left to walk along the bank, with the river Eau on your left. Continue all the way to the road, passing the old tramcar body on the right just before you reach the road. Turn left down the road back to your starting place.

26 Nettleton
The Salutation Inn

Commanding the crossroads at the foot of Caistor Brow on the main Grimsby road, the Salutation Inn stands on a site where locals and travellers have sought refreshment probably since Roman times, when the nearby ironstone mines were worked, although the present building only dates from the 19th century. This pleasant real-ale hostelry is full of character and situated in a village that also goes back hundreds of years, with parts of the church dating from the late Saxon era.

Recently completely altered and re-furbished, the inn has an attractive carpeted L-shaped lounge, with a delightfully light and airy dining room at one end. In addition, there is a separate restaurant capable of seating 30 people. The decor throughout is notable for its warm colours and good quality furniture and pictures. The inn is well used by local people and, if you are fortunate, you may meet Alan Tailby, the artist responsible for some of the sketches on the wall. There is also an outdoor fenced play area and picnic place to the rear of the inn.

Vivien and John Gibbon extend a warm welcome to all who call to drink and dine and their extensive menu includes home-made soup, pâté, crispy mushrooms and loaded potato skins for starters. There are seasonal mixed salads with warm crusty bread, and main course platters range from old-fashioned omelette, gypsy stew, whole plaice mariner style to vegetable stir fry. Children may select a smaller portion from any of the starred dishes on the menu. Whitbread Trophy Bitter, Boddingtons Mild, Boddingtons Bitter, Flowers Original and Fuller's London Pride are among the real ales on offer and each week there is a guest beer such as Morland Old Speckled Hen. Copperhead, Old English and Addlestone's cask conditioned cider, Stella Artois and Heineken lagers and wine on tap are also available.

The pub is open on Monday to Saturday from 11.30 am to 3 pm and 6 pm to 11 pm (all day on a summer Saturday), and on Sunday from 12 noon to 10.30 pm. Meals are served from 12 noon until 2 pm and from 7 pm until 9.45 pm, and often at weekends it is wise to book restaurant meals in advance.

Telephone: 01472 851228.

How to get there: The inn is situated on the A46 Lincoln to Grimsby road, 7 miles north of Market Rasen or 13 miles south of Grimsby.

Parking: There is a large car park and limited roadside parking is possible in the immediate vicinity but not in the village itself.

Length of the walk: 4 miles. Map: OS Landranger sheet 113 Grimsby and surrounding area (inn GR 109002).

A stroll up the historic Nettleton valley with medieval village sites in an Area of Outstanding Natural Beauty and a steepish uphill stretch with some marvellous views that illustrate, quite dramatically, that Lincolnshire is certainly not flat. You may find some mud at field entrances, so go well shod.

The Walk

Leave the main road to turn left out of the car park up Church Street into the village, with the post office on your right. Walk past the ancient, weather-worn church and round the bend in the road to the right towards Normanby le Wold, for around ½ mile.

Turn left up the signposted track with bridleway signpost and Viking Way waymarks, to walk past Nettleton Grange Farm on your right. Bear left on the track by the farm buildings to the white metal fieldgate and the commemorative oak ladder stile. This is the junction of three local long distance paths, the Viking Way, the Nev Cole Way and Lindsey Loop.

Turn right over the Countryside Commission Stewardship land,

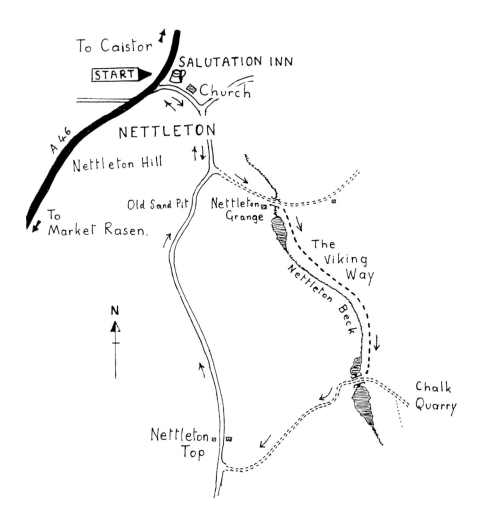

To Caistor

START

SALUTATION INN

Church

A 46

NETTLETON

Nettleton Hill

Old Sand Pit

Nettleton Grange

The Viking Way

Nettleton Beck

To Market Rasen.

N

Nettleton Top

Chalk Quarry

which gives unlimited access, to walk up the valley, keeping the beck and the large pond on your right. For a few yards it is often rather boggy on this stretch. Cross the footbridge and stile and then two other stiles and, upon reaching the crosstrack halfway up the Nettleton valley, climb the stile by the side of the metal fieldgate and turn immediately right, downhill, along the deteriorating concrete track that was formerly the road leading into the quarry.

Cross the bridge between the two ponds and climb steeply uphill along the old quarry road, with an occasional pause to look at the wonderful panorama. Climb three stiles and upon reaching the Normanby road by Nettleton Top Farm, with its wide road verges, turn right, downhill, all the way back into the village.

Other places of interest: Nettleton Wood, near Caistor, is a 25-acre area a short walk from the A46, lying just below the edge of the Wolds. It is partly covered by woodland with areas of heath and grassland.

Barnoldby le Bec
The Ship Inn

27

This roadside pub serves the small village of Barnoldby le Bec and travellers to and from Waltham and beyond. Like several villages in this area, Barnoldby had strong Quaker connections and many Quaker families from hereabouts sailed from the nearby Immingham Creek in 1603 on their trip first to Plymouth and then, aboard the *Mayflower*, to land at Cape Cod to found a settlement that eventually became Massachusetts.

The Ship, therefore, has some connections with the sea and a ship's bell is rung at closing time. There are attractive sea prints on the walls and a ship's steering wheel in the after-cabin part of the lounge. There is a blackboard menu that alters frequently according to the season, and the pub's proximity to the port of Grimsby means that the fish for the various fish dishes comes straight from the trawlers. A favourite dish, though, is the Ship Inn Special Hot Beef – a slice of bread fried in beef dripping, topped with layers of topside beef and a rich beer and onion gravy. There is a selection of salads and freshly made sandwiches, including smoked salmon and a choice of white or brown bread. The cosy 26-seater dining-room is a no-smoking area. Charles Gillis, the landlord, serves his own choice of beer and Flowers

Original, Theakston Best Bitter and Donnington Bitter are served from handpumps, along with Stella Artois and Heineken lagers. Draught Guinness, Murphy's Irish Stout and Strongbow cider complete the range of drinks on offer. There is a pleasant area at the rear laid out with picnic tables and, in season, bedecked with flowers in tubs and hanging baskets.

The pub is open on Monday to Saturday from 11 am to 3 pm and 6.30 pm to 11 pm, and on Sunday from 12 noon to 3 pm and 7 pm to 10.30 pm. Meals are available each day from 12 noon to 2 pm and 7 pm to 9.30 pm.

Telephone: 0472 822308.

How to get there: Turn off the A46 Grimsby to Caistor road at the junction with the A18 (T) road on Laceby roundabout and follow the B1431 for 2½ miles before turning down into Barnoldby le Bec.

Parking: Customers may park in one of the two car parks at the Ship, with the permission of the landlord. There is really no suitable alternative parking in the immediate vicinity although, by extending the route, it would be possible to use the car park in Bradley Woods and to interrupt your walk for refreshment by calling at the Ship.

Length of the walk: 4 easy miles. Map: OS Landranger sheet 113 Grimsby and surrounding area (inn GR 235032).

A pleasant, peaceful countryside stroll, almost entirely along good track and field boundaries, walking through the flat lands leading down to the Humber Estuary some 5 miles away. Barton Street Roman road, the 'cliff-edge' of the Wolds and the woods at Bradley are in view and the magnificent six-sailed windmill at Waltham can be seen across the fields. It is a working landscape and big sky country that is well worth exploring.

The Walk

Turn right out of the car park and immediately right again up Chapel Lane, signposted 'bridleway' with a waymark for the Wanderlust Way (WW). Walk forward, with the church on your left and after reading the inscription on the obelisk to the right, past Glebe Farm Cottage and with Waltham windmill in view from this section of the walk.

At Low Farm track junction continue to walk forward towards Bradley Woods on the bridleway, with a hedge on your left, for 200 yards. Turn left off the bridleway onto a signposted footpath at the end of the reservoir (this path has been officially diverted but it may not be as indicated on your OS map). Follow the path, with the reservoir on your left at first. Continue on the track round to the right

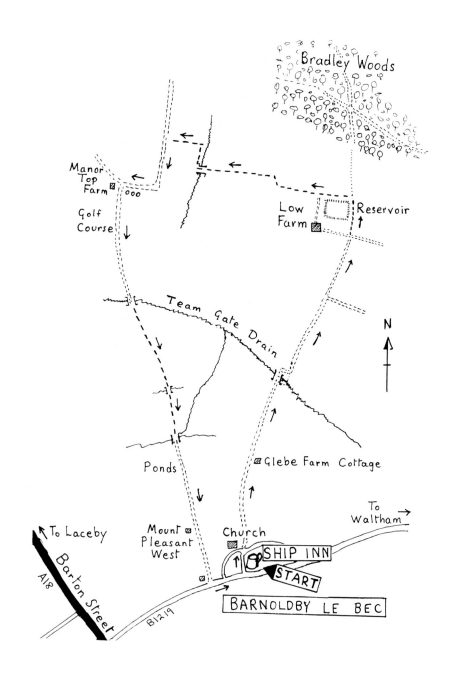

for 30 yards (do not go through the fieldgate) to turn left, with a fence on the left and a hedge on the right, and continue until you reach the footbridge.

Cross the bridge and then turn right along the field edge for another 30 yards, before turning left along the field boundary, with an old hedgeline and trees on your left. Go over the earth bridge and turn left along the good wide track towards Manor Top Farm with its three green silos. Turn left at the farm and keep to the left track with a golf course on your immediate right. Follow this track until you reach Team Gate Drain.

Cross the bridge and proceed diagonally left on a defined path until you meet a footbridge over a side dyke. Walk straight forward from the bridge across the next field to a track, with the hedge on the left, leading up to Mount Pleasant West. There are ponds and islands over on the right. Continue down this path to the road and then turn left to your starting place, after observing the date on the manor house across the road.

Other places of interest: Bradley Woods with its picnic area and car parking is owned by Grimsby Borough Council and you are free to wander at will. A plaque explains that it is the start of the Wanderlust Way, a 20-mile circular route created as a tribute to Nev Cole, a well-loved local rambler.

Burton upon Stather
The Sheffield Arms

A welcoming, friendly place, this old inn was built in 1664 and at one time was known as the Black Bull. It was renamed the Sheffield Arms out of respect for the Sheffield family who have been important landowners in the area since the 16th century. The most illustrious member of the Sheffield family was John Sheffield, third Earl of Mulgrave, who intrigued at court. Charles II made him a captain at sea and a colonel on land. King James made him Lord Chamberlain, King William made him Marquis of Normanby and Queen Anne Lord Privy Seal and Duke of Buckingham. The ancient ferry plying from Stather to Garthorpe was part of a route used by King's messengers, who had to be given passage on demand. The ferry also carried passengers and was used for carrying sheep bound for Wakefield Market. During the Second World War units practised here with secret waterproofed tanks, preparing for the Rhine crossing.

The inn is an imposing building right at the end of the high street, adjacent to the church, and has always been important to the prosperity of the village. It has been carefully refurbished and now the bars have all the comfort you could ask for, but have lost none of their old appeal. An L-shaped bar serves the old, beamed lounge, with its panelling and comfortable settle seating. There are brasses and paintings decorating the walls and an interesting map of the area. A tied house, it serves Wards bitter and other of the brewery's beers. The meals are really something special, with a bar menu ranging from giant Yorkshire pudding with onion gravy, home-made steak and kidney pie, baked ham and peaches, and bacon steak with pineapple to half a roast chicken. There is a selection of cold meats and fish dishes and six types of sandwiches, both hot and cold. Various salads can be made to order. On Thursdays, Fridays and Saturdays there is a notice board announcing a 'Special of the Day'. Children under the age of 14 cannot be catered for in the public house. There is a separate section of the lounge for dining and a small patio area at the rear.

The inn is open on Monday to Saturday from 11.30 am to 3 pm and 7 pm to 11 pm, and on Sunday from 12 noon to 3 pm and 7 pm to 10.30 pm. Meals are served from 12 noon to 2 pm and from 7 pm to 10.30 pm (not Sunday evenings).

Telephone: 01724 720269.

How to get there: Burton upon Stather is 5 miles north of Scunthorpe on the B1340, signposted as a scenic route. Alternatively, turn off the A1077 road at Winterton, going to Thealby and then on to Burton upon Stather.

Parking: Customers may park in the Sheffield Arms car park while they are doing the walk. No other suitable parking is available in the immediate vicinity. However, it would be possible to park at the picnic place near the water tower shown on the sketch map and to visit the Sheffield Arms en route.

Length of the walk: 3 miles. Map: OS Landranger sheet 112 Scunthorpe (inn GR 870179).

Wonderful, totally unexpected views across the river Trent over the green Isle of Axholme and, if conditions are suitable, right across Yorkshire to York Minster. At 200 ft above sea level, the 'upon' of Burton upon Stather signifies that the village is situated above the river Trent and not on it. This was the land of the Vikings and Stather is derived from 'stoth' or 'staithe', meaning 'a landing place' in Old Norse.

The Walk

From the car park walk down the narrow passage to the left of the hotel into Main Street and continue down the road, with the post office on your right. At the bend leave Main Street to follow the signposted, tarmac footpath on the right. Turn right upon reaching the

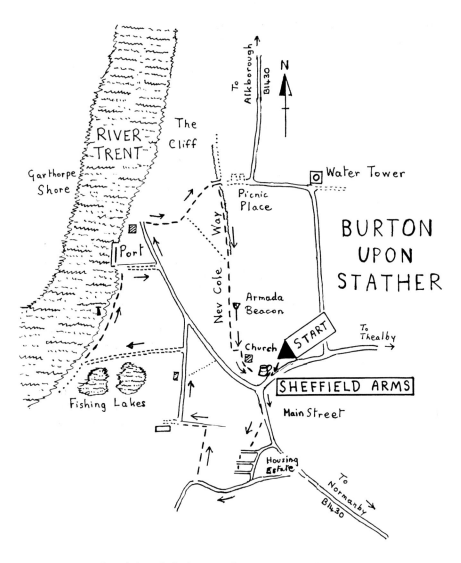

estate road and then left along a clear tarmac path between the houses, crossing estate roads until you reach Westover Drive, where you cannot go any further forward. Turn left up the drive and, at the T-junction, right until you reach the lane.

Turn right, downhill, along the steep, narrow lane. At the bottom of the hill, where it turns sharp left, climb the stile on the right and follow a clear path across the rough grazing field almost to the hedge on the far side. Turn left downhill to the signpost and stile in the right-hand corner of the field. Climb the stile and turn right up the lane, leaving the sewage plant behind you.

About 175 yards past the farmhouse on your left, turn left down a good track, with large fishing ponds on your left. Turn right upon reaching the river bank, along the raised flood control embankment, past the navigation beacon. Upon reaching the port complex, turn right down a clear path to the road. Turn left at the road with the Ferry House Inn and Kings Ferry House on your left, and then right up the signposted path, going steeply uphill. Ignore the first footpath on the right halfway up the hill and proceed to the top.

Turn right by the footbridge leading to the car park, with the drain on your left. Walk on past the Armada Beacon and turn left up the narrow path to the churchyard, shortly after passing the kissing-gate. To the west of the churchyard wall is the site of the ancient market. A Tuesday market was chartered by the Earl of Lancaster in 1315. Turn into the churchyard and walk past the 13th century, much-restored church to the car park at the Sheffield Arms on your left. Have a look at the lovely doorway of the church and, if it is open, do take time to go inside to view the many monuments to the Sheffield family.

Other places of interest: Normanby Hall Country Park is only a couple of miles away and is well worth a visit. It has 350 acres of beautiful parkland and gardens surrounding a Regency country house, once the home of the Sheffields. There is a country centre with nature trails and guided walks through the deer park, woodlands and gardens. Other attractions include wild and ornamental birds, craft workshops, a farming museum, golf course and fishing lake. An admission fee is charged. If you need more details, ring 01724 720588.

㉙ **Barrow Haven**
The Haven Inn

Barrow Haven is an ancient place, for the green mounds known as The Castles, on a good strategic position by the beck, are the extensive remains of a great Saxon or Danish earthwork, covering eight acres. Just 4 miles away, at the hamlet of Burnham, legend sites the historically important Battle of Brunanburh where King Athelstan routed the enemies of Wessex, killing five kings and establishing the unity of England. Today though, Barrow Haven is a small port dealing mainly in Scandinavian timber with an odd little railway station on a branch line that actually still functions.

Jenny and David Strange have created a comfortably modernised pub with an emphasis on good food. The inn was built in the 1740s and until the late 1800s offered accommodation and hospitality to passengers to and from the Humber Ferry, sailing at that time from Barrow Haven. It is a freehouse, with well-kept John Smith's, Directors and guest ales. Strongbow cider is also available and lagers. The extensive menu offers excellent home-cooked meals, with a range from beefburgers to beef Wellington. There is a good vegetarian menu and varied home-made pies. Members of staff and their various roles are given, which is a nice personal touch. There is a garden area for children, a large games room with a dartboard and pool table and a pleasant, separate restaurant. Nine en suite rooms are available for overnight accommodation. Children are welcome in all areas except the public bar. Dogs are not permitted indoors, except in bedrooms.

The inn is open from 11 am to 11 pm on Monday to Friday, 11 am to 3 pm and 7 pm to 11 pm on Saturday and 12 noon to 3 pm and 7 pm to 10.30 pm on Sunday. Meals are served daily from 12 noon to 2 pm, and from 7 pm to 9.30 pm.

Telephone: 01469 530247.

How to get there: Turn off the A1077 Barton upon Humber – Barrow upon Humber road at a very sharp right-angled bend where it is signposted 'Barrow Haven'. The pub is almost 1 mile down this lane.

Parking: Customers may park in the very large car park of the Haven Inn, or it would be possible to park on the roadside near the railway crossing, north of the inn.

Length of the walk: 2 miles. Map: OS Landranger sheet 112 Scunthorpe (inn GR 062230).

A walk for bird lovers, for this stroll explores a remote nature reserve on the Humber Bank, with a splendid view upstream of the world-renowned bridge that has a beauty all of its own. New breeding species of birds for this area, such as the greylag goose, ruddy duck or possibly the sparrowhawk may be seen, while Canada geese, collared doves and lesser whitethroats have increased in these old clay pit reserves.

The Walk

Turn left out of the inn car park to walk along the road for 700 yards, with the drain embankment on your left. Turn left at the railway bridge over the tidal drain and immediately right into Barrow Haven Reedbed Nature Reserve. The steps on the left of the path lead down to a bird-watching hide that you may wish to explore but it is a cul-de-sac. Take the waymarked path down to the kissing-gate on the left, to turn left by the concrete jetty and the sunken barge, away from the Humber Bank path.

Follow this good track, with the waterski club on your right and an extensive reedbed on the left. Go through the handgate and the two railway gates at the level crossing and continue down the long straight section of West Marsh Lane to eventually follow the lane round the bends to the left, over the road bridge and past the old mill back to the Haven Inn.

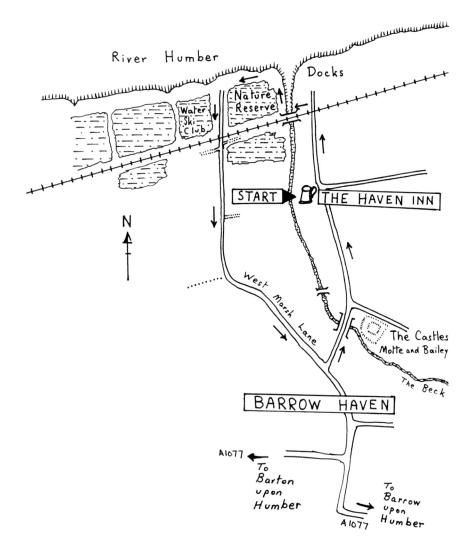

Other places of interest: The Humber Bridge has a viewing area, free parking and toilets and a picnic area. It is well signed through Barton upon Humber. The bridge was, before the Ma Wan Channel Bridge in Hong Kong, the longest single span suspension bridge in the world. The clearance over the water is 98 ft and the total length between anchorages is 1.38 miles. There is an exhilarating walk over the bridge and a bus service.

Far Ings Nature Reserve. A walkway from the viewing area has shallow and deep water area, reedbeds, woodland and well maintained pathways. There are explanatory leaflets.

East Halton
The Black Bull

East Halton, once solely a farming community in the flat lands away from the coast, has now grown into a large village with the development of the nearby North Killingholme Haven oil terminal on the Humber Bank.

The Black Bull is a friendly local pub, much frequented by members of the farming community. It has a U-shaped bar, with a games annexe that includes a pool table and a dartboard. There is a very comfortable lounge bar at the rear, with plush seating, brown decor and old variety act prints on the wall, and a pleasant garden area for children is outside.

The bar menu includes The Bull's Pat – Yorkshire pudding with onion gravy – and the Bull's Filled Pat with beef and Lincolnshire sausage, Hungarian beef goulash, Greek moussaka, lasagne verdi, chicken dishes, Dublin Bay scampi, lemon sole goujons, tuna and pasta bake and seafood lasagne. Vegetarian dishes such as broccoli and cream cheese pie or vegetable lasagne are also on offer. There is a blackboard menu for each day's special dish, fisherman's pie being an example. This is a Marston's house, serving real ales, and an extensive range of beers is available. Ansells Mild, John Smith's Bitter and

Marston's Pedigree Bitter are among the beers, and Kronenbourg 1664, Tennents Extra and Carlsberg are the lagers. Draught Guinness and Murphy's Stout and three ciders, Scrumpy Jack, Dry Blackthorn and Taunton Autumn Gold are also on offer.

The pub is open on Monday to Saturday from 11 am to 11 pm, and on Sunday from 12 noon to 3 pm and 7 pm to 10.30 pm. Meals are available from 12 noon until 2.30 pm and from 7 pm until 10 pm.

Telephone: 01469 540207.

How to get there: From the A160, which runs from the A180, Brigg to Grimsby road, to the coast, north-west of Grimsby, turn north at South Killingholme and go through North Killingholme to East Halton.

Parking: Customers may park in the Black Bull car park. There is alternative roadside parking in the immediate vicinity.

Length of the walk: 4¼ miles. Map: OS Landranger sheet 113, Grimsby and surrounding area (inn GR 139195).

East Halton is a little village of the byways, only a couple of miles from the Humber. The fine remains of Thornton Abbey on East Halton Beck are part of the walk. The abbey was founded by the Lord of Holderness in 1139 and, after the Dissolution of the Monasteries, Henry VIII held his court there for three days in 1541. It once covered 100 acres and was surrounded by a wall and a moat, the remains of which bear testimony to its former magnificence. Today the splendid gatehouse, built of stone and brick and standing 50 ft high, is an obvious photographic souvenir of a pleasant walk.

The Walk

Turn right out of the pub car park and walk along the road for 350 yards, then right down the signposted farm track almost opposite Swinster Lane. Follow this clear track for 1 mile and, on reaching the path junction by the hedge, go through the wooden fieldgate and turn right along the good track, with the hedge on your right and the abbey over on your left across the field.

Turn left at the road for 350 yards and, at the sharp bend in the road, turn left at the end of the metal crash barrier, through the double metal fieldgate. Take the clear footpath, with East Halton Beck on your right, to the splendid new bridge with stile and gate. Cross the bridge and walk on to a smaller second footbridge, going forward, with the fence on your left, and down the steps to the road. Turn left at the road to the abbey, where there is a picnic place outside which would be a good apple stop.

Thornton Abbey is open daily from 1 April to 30 September

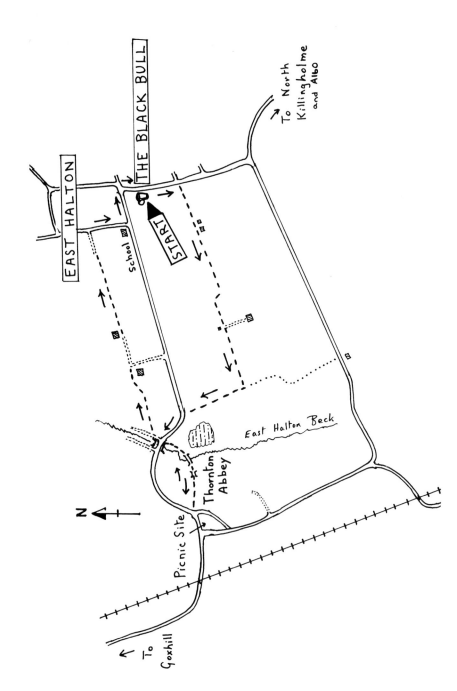

THE BLACK BULL

EAST HALTON

To North Killingholme and Albo

School

START

East Halton Beck

Thornton Abbey

Picnic Site

N

To Goxhill

(10 am – 6 pm) and at weekends (10 am – 4 pm) during the rest of the year. Members of English Heritage free, otherwise there is an admission charge. After viewing (and photographing) the abbey, retrace your steps from the picnic site as far as the crash barrier at the bend of the road. Cross the road with care and after a few yards turn right down the track, with East Halton Beck on your left and a small dyke on the right.

Cross the footbridge, or alternatively go through the wooden fieldgate, to follow the clearly defined path across the two fields, aiming for the left-hand side of the farm buildings. Follow the path round the farm buildings to the right and then turn left on reaching the straight green lane, which leads you past a rehabilitated farmhouse to the road. Turn right at the road and, upon reaching the junction with the main road with the school on your right, turn left up the main road and then right at the road junction, back to the Black Bull.